GREATER
MEN AND WOMEN
OF THE BIBLE

GREATER

MEN AND WOMEN

OF THE BIBLE

By

Will Sessions

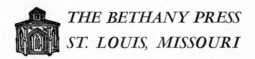

THE BETHANY PRESS
ST. LOUIS, MISSOURI

Scripture quotations, unless otherwise noted, are from the *Revised Standard Version of the Bible,* copyrighted 1946 and 1952 by the Division of Christian Education, National Council of Churches of Christ in the United States of America, and used by permission.

Library of Congress Catalog Card Number: 58-7478

Second printing 1958

Printed in the United States of America

Preface

One of the great contributions of the Bible is that it brings to life, in a very realistic manner, all kinds and conditions of people. Here we find people as they really are, saints and sinners, and sometimes a mixture of both. The strength of this book by Dr. Sessions is that it takes the great characters of the Old and New Testaments just as they are, bringing them into focus and giving background material which often sheds new light upon familiar individuals.

The Bible is a wonderful book of theology. It has in it the words of life. History, poetry, drama, stories, the gospel narrative are all found within its covers. Yet the Bible would not mean nearly as much today if it were not for the personalities which walk up and down upon its creative pages. This is what brings the book to life. We appreciate the value of the Ten Commandments, but it is the story of Moses that makes them real. There are great moral and spiritual lessons in the books of the prophets, but it is the prophets themselves who challenge us to higher moral and spiritual endeavor. In the New Testament we have the gospel story itself revealed in five different forms, yet it is what happened to Matthew, Mark, Luke, John and Paul, as the result of meeting Christ, that makes the New Testament a living book.

So it is with Christ himself. His teachings and his spirit are of the divine. But separated from his sacrificial life they would not mean so much to us today. Moreover, many of his greatest teachings developed directly out of his life—out of his daily living. His contacts and conversations with other people, par-

5

ticularly with the disciples, served as channels for words and parables which have been cherished down through the centuries.

What I like especially about this book is the freshness with which Dr. Sessions approaches such a large number of prominent men and women of the whole Bible. He has let them speak for themselves, without loading them down with a lot of interpretations. As a result we have here brief character studies which appeal to all age groups, and which can be used in various ways from the pulpit, in the church school, and in the home. Because the book is composed of Bible characters, it can be used over a long period of time, both for reference and for inspiration.

Personally I have profited spiritually by reading this material in manuscript form. Now that it is in book form, I am sure that many readers will profit similarly as they share the experiences, human and divine, of these men and women of the Bible.

Stanley I. Stuber
Kansas City, Missouri

Contents

Adam

Time: *Biblically reckoned by some at about 4000* B.C.

Place: *Garden of Eden which is supposed to have been between the Tigris and the Euphrates rivers in Mesopotamia.*

Scripture: *Genesis 1:26—5:15; Matthew 19:4-6; Mark 10:6-8; Luke 3:3-8; Romans 5:12-21; 1 Corinthians 15:22, 44-47; Philippians 2:6; 1 Timothy 2:13-15*

One of the obvious things about the New Testament is the fact that the first four books—Matthew, Mark, Luke, and John—are biographies of the life of our Lord. The careful student will discover that each of those writers has told a slightly differing story, each remembered some incident or referred to some happening with a slightly different emphasis, yet the combined work of the four gives a rounded picture of the life and the teachings of Jesus.

It should not, then, surprise any student of the Old Testament to learn that there are actually two accounts of the creation in the one Book of Genesis. As to whether Moses, a matchless scholar and a man of tremendous learning, wove the stories, which were over a thousand years old, into the pattern that we find in Genesis, or whether some scribe had already done that so that Moses simply copied an earlier work, remains a question. Such is the problem that scholars face in their effort to learn how the manuscript came into being.

Genesis 1:27 reads "God created man in his own image, in the image of God he created him; male and female he created them." In Genesis 2:7 we are told that the LORD God formed man of the dust from the ground. When it was found that it was not good for man to be alone, the LORD God caused a deep sleep to fall upon Adam and, while he slept, took one of his ribs, closed up the flesh, and made a woman and brought her to the man. (Verses 21-22.) In the first instance the Godhead is referred to as God; in the second account as the LORD God.

Very distinctly the text says that Adam was formed of the dust from the ground, and inasmuch as all of us are made of the same elements it can be concluded that we are as dust and shall return to dust. (Genesis 3:19.)

That section of the story which deals with Eve being created from the rib of Adam is particularly interesting since there is little accounting for the source from which the Hebrews acquired such an idea. If men had one less rib than women, this idea would have had speculative foundation; but the fact that men have the same number of ribs on both sides of their bodies and that women have the same number as men makes it difficult to find at what point in the thinking of the early people that idea had its beginning.

Adam was never regarded as a paleolithic creature. He may have been the last object of creation in a long process of the separation of the earth from the waters and of the light from the darkness and of making the creatures move about upon the face of the earth, but it was never thought that man as such was the result of that process. Adam was never thought of as having evolved but rather as being a special creation, distinct and apart.

That he was created in the image of God according to the text has been the foundation for the thinking that God has a face, hands, arms, and all the physical characteristics of man. God has been thought of as a sort of superman who moved from place to place. That is not our thought, however, when we say, "In the image of God he created him," for we think in terms of the spiritual similarities. It is that God's Spirit and man's spirit are akin. To be like God's image in a spiritual sense ap-

10

peals to us because we read, "God is spirit, and those who worship him must worship in spirit and truth." (John 4:24.)

Eden was a sort of paradise which according to the archeologists is said to have been between the Tigris and Euphrates rivers in that area that is known as Mesopotamia, which literally means "between the rivers." This idyllic Garden was a very wonderful place to the Hebrews. They thought of it as a spot of unsurpassed beauty and innocence. The knowledge of Adam and Eve was very limited. The restriction that was set before them was that they should not acquire knowledge of good and evil. We are prone to think of it as being that they were not to learn about evil only. Adam was to live in the Garden. There was to be no sweat of the brow, no constructive labor of any sort whatsoever. There was no need for improving his condition until he was thrust out.

Two tremendously important trees grew in Eden. One was the tree of the knowledge of good and evil. It was the act of acquiring this knowledge that brought about the expulsion. (Genesis 2:16-17.) Apparently the punishment for learning was nothing less than death itself. Paul's statement to the Corinthians is linked with this when he says, "For as by a man came death, by a man has come also the resurrection of the dead. For as in Adam all die, so also in Christ shall all be made alive." (1 Corinthians 15:21-22.) Very definitely in Hebrew thought death was linked with Adam's daring to eat of the forbidden fruit of the tree of knowledge. The second tree, the tree of life, seems to have been forbidden to man's appetite also, for the text distinctly says that Adam and Eve were driven from the Garden because the LORD God was concerned "lest he [the man] put forth his hand and take also of the tree of life, and eat, and live for ever." (Genesis 3:22.)

Some people today feel that the ultimate proof of God's existence is that man has never been able to learn the secret of creating life. There is a feeling that to know this would mean that man would have become equal with God. This position is dangerous for one's faith since creation of life is but one of

11

the infinitude of mysteries that surround the very nature of God.

Adam was charged with the naming of the birds, the beasts, the entire creation. The LORD God brought them before Adam to see what he would call them, and "whatever the man called every living creature that was its name." (Genesis 2:19.) Actually some modification of this process has been going on through all the centuries from that time till now, for it is ever man who names the animals, the birds, the things about him.

Once he was driven from Eden, punishment was inflicted upon Adam. It was stipulated that he would have "to till the ground from which he was taken." (Genesis 3:23.)

Adam stands a towering figure as the progenitor of all mankind from whom all races, tribes, and peoples are descended. It was at the mature age of nine hundred and thirty years that he died. (Genesis 5:5.)

Eve

Time: *Biblically reckoned by some at about 4000* B.C.

Place: *Garden of Eden which is supposed to have been between the Tigris and Euphrates rivers in Mesopotamia*

Scripture: *Genesis 2:18—4:26; 2 Corinthians 11:3; 1 Timothy 2:13-15*

✗ Eve, often referred to as Mother Eve, began her life as an afterthought of creation. Man was created in the likeness of God, but it was found that it was not good for him to be alone. (Genesis 2:18.) As a result of this compelling need for companionship, it was decided to create an associate—one who would meet this social need of man, and at the same time be a helpmeet for him.

✗ Just as Adam himself had been without father or mother but came from the very dust of the ground at the creative will of God, so Eve was without father or mother but came from the rib that God extracted from Adam's side when he was in a deep sleep.

✗ When Adam saw her, he gave her two names. In one instance she was to be called "Woman" because she was taken out of man. (Genesis 2:33.) Then in the second instance she was called "Eve" because she was the mother of all living. (Genesis 3:20.) Both names have stayed through the centuries and while all womankind bears the first name, Eve personally retains the second title.

That Adam and Eve found great joy in their companionship may be clearly inferred from the Scripture. They were so rightly a part of life in their need for each other that the biblical conclusion is that a man will leave his father and mother to cleave to his wife, and that "they shall become one flesh." (Genesis 2:24.)

Snakes are usually not favorite pets. Women have been afraid of them in all generations, and apparently this antipathy is traced back to Eve's early encounter with the serpent. One is led to believe that there was such a multiplicity of everything that was good and satisfying in the Garden of Eden that there was nothing for which anyone could long, and yet because the fruit of the tree of the knowledge of good and evil was forbidden, the temptation to eat of it became intolerable. The serpent, gifted with the power of speech, urged her to taste the fruit of the tree, and gave reasons for doing so.

Notice that one is swept along with the story and thinks that the serpent is Satan or the Devil, yet there is no such statement in the record. The serpent is a serpent from beginning to end. Compare the opening chapter of Job where Satan is specifically called Satan. The serpent simply prodded the curiosity of the woman, who yielded to the temptation, ate the fruit herself, then persuaded Adam.

This may indicate that woman's daring and adventurous spirit is actually greater than man's. That statement may not be too popular with some men.

When the text says that their eyes were opened, the meaning is purely figurative because the conversation with the Lord God makes it clear that they had eyesight before. What happened to them was a matter of understanding rather than of sight, for the Lord God asked: "Who told you that you were naked?" Not "Who opened your eyes?" (Genesis 3:11.)

Then, although Eve tried to say that she was beguiled by the serpent, the Lord God made it perfectly clear that they were to be punished just the same. As for the serpent, the Lord God said that the serpent shall crawl upon its belly and that there shall always be particular enmity between serpents and humans.

14

As for the woman, Eve, the LORD God said,

"I will greatly multiply your pain in childbearing;
in pain you shall bring forth children."—Genesis 3:16.

A tremendous number of people still feel that it is a sin to interfere with the pains of childbirth, and that any use of anesthetic aids in times of labor is sinful, that by rights woman should bring forth her children in pain and sorrow, all due to this punishment upon Eve.

Mother Eve must get her name from the fact that she was the first mother rather than from the fact that she was the mother of a large family, for according to the account she gave birth to three sons, Cain (Genesis 4:1), Abel (Genesis 4:2), and Seth (Genesis 4:25). There may have been other children, to be sure, both sons and daughters, but if so their names do not appear. Cain and Abel are the better known of the three. The very thought of Eve bringing her young into the world without the aid of an obstetrician, and then of her being able to manage without special formulas seems almost too wonderful to believe, and yet that dreadfully handicapped first mother succeeded in rearing her sons to manhood.

The fact that the woman shall be inordinately drawn to the man so that, as the text puts it,

Your desire shall be for your husband,
and he shall rule over you

appears rather ignominious. Woman's position thereby becomes definitely subservient, and she becomes the victim of her own attachment for the man she loves.

15

Cain

Father: *Adam*

Mother: *Eve*

Time: *Biblically reckoned by some at about 4000* B.C.

Place: *Near to the Garden of Eden, the land of Nod, and the territory in and around Mesopotamia*

Scripture: *Genesis 4:1-11; 1 John 3:12; Jude 11*

The name of Cain is inseparably linked with that of Abel. Of the two boys Cain was the elder. (Genesis 4:1-2.)

One never quite stops to realize that here were the members of a small family with Adam as the father and Eve as the mother, and that one of the sons became a juvenile delinquent. Just what failure in the parental guidance of Adam and Eve prevented the two sons from loving one another is unknown.

Abel was a keeper of sheep, and sheepherders in all generations since have been a problem to the tillers of the soil. Those men who raise crops do not like to have animals roaming all over their fields. No mention is made of this offense in the text, for the text focuses on the matter of the offerings. "The LORD had regard for Abel and his offering, but for Cain and his offering he had no regard." (Genesis 4:4b and 5a.) Just what that regard involved is a matter of conjecture.

The green-eyed monster of jealousy rose between the two, and it raged into a fury while they were in the field, with the result that Cain slew Abel. (Genesis 4:8.) Thus we have right at the beginning of humankind the angers, the tempers, the conflicts that have grown into larger proportions through the centuries, until now we have the devastating wars, the efforts at understanding ownership and one another's rights, that shake the very foundations of society. There was no court, there was no trial, there was no penitentiary.

It is interesting that Adam and Eve did not enter into the picture to censure or to blame. Adam did not say to his son, "This is a sin, my boy." No, it was the LORD who sought Cain and who brought him to task for what he had done. "Where is Abel thy brother?" he asked. Then Cain set forth a question that has been a poser for every generation from his time to the present, "Am I my brother's keeper?"

The LORD made no direct answer to this. He said that the voice of Abel's blood was crying from the ground and that the earth would be cursed, and that Cain would be cursed as long as he lived because of the sin he committed. "When you till the ground, it shall no longer yield to you its strength; you shall be a fugitive and a wanderer on the earth." (Genesis 4:12.)

Just how Cain could contend with God and hope to win is a question, but Cain said, "My punishment is greater than I can bear." And he cried out against the suffering that was to be his. It is worth noting that Cain blamed God for the business. "Behold, thou hast driven me this day away from the ground; and from thy face I shall be hidden." Then Cain ended his appeal by saying that eventually he would be killed.

This seems to have been beyond the expectation of God, and he set a mark upon Cain as a protective symbol "lest any who came upon him should kill him." Just what this symbol may have been is not mentioned, and seemingly no records give any trace of what it was.

Cain was the father of only one son so far as the record tells. His name was Enoch.

As in the case of Eve, no mention is made of Cain's death, no record of how long he lived or where he was buried.

Noah

Father: *Lamech*

Mother: *Not known*

Time: *Approximately 2500 B.C.*

Place: *Mesopotamia*

Scripture: *Genesis 5:28—9:29; Luke 3:36; Hebrews 11:17*

One of the most beloved and most admired characters of the Bible is Noah. Not every man would have had the courage to build an ark in the midst of a dry land. Noah was the only one of his time who had the foresight to see that the flood was coming and who prepared for himself, his family, his cattle, and his fowl against the eventuality of the catastrophe.

Noah was born to Lamech. (Genesis 5:28.) As to his mother's name, or as to the name of his wife or of his sons' wives, there is no mention. They are called "wives" and nothing more. This may indicate the rather indifferent status of women in that day, or it may simply be that the men so overshadowed the women that their names have been forgotten.

There is something pathetic in the fact that the condition of mankind should have sunk to such depths that it would be written, "Every imagination of the thoughts of his heart was only evil continually." (Genesis 6:5.) Little wonder that it should have grieved the Lord that he created mankind. Apparently with his sinfulness man had broken the heart of God, and God decided to wipe the face of the earth clean. (Genesis 6:7.)

That he should have spared Noah is surprising, but Noah and his family were upright and the LORD decided to save them. (Genesis 6:13.)

The heroism of this man is magnificent. It took courage in the face of ridicule and sporting jibes to build so monstrous a boat in the midst of barren land. Although anyone could see how he might have formed a raft of some 450 feet (Genesis 6:15), and although he might have built a three-story barn on it (Genesis 6:16), the fact that he would have been able to build a boat after the manner that we know, a boat of three hundred cubits, is amazing indeed. Apparently it was without a rudder, without any means of self-propulsion. What kept it from being swept downstream to the sea is incomprehensible. Just as we have to say with a lot of these things, the hand of the LORD was at work.

In Genesis 6:19 Noah was told that he was to take the animals "two of every sort" into the ark. Yet a few verses further he was told that he should take seven pairs of the clean beasts, seven pairs of the fowls, but only pairs of the unclean. (Genesis 7:2-3.) Then we read that Noah went into the ark with his sons, his wife, and his sons' wives with him (Genesis 7:7), yet shortly we repeat that "On the very same day Noah and his sons, Shem and Ham and Japheth, and Noah's wife, and the three wives of his sons with them entered the ark." (Genesis 7:13.) This sounds a little redundant, until it is viewed in the light of what the scholars have to say, namely, that this is a blending of two stories of Noah's miraculous deliverance. This has been mentioned already in the account of Adam and the problems of the creation. It is a reasonable approach and helps in understanding the text.

For forty days and forty nights it rained, and the water covered everything in sight. The water covered the highest mountains of the earth, and for years the presence of tiny fossils in the rock formations of those mountains thousands of feet above sea level, was taken as affirmation of the flood covering the earth.

19

One hundred and fifty days the waters prevailed upon the earth. (Genesis 7:24.) This would mean that there was flood for approximately five months, which is a terrifically long period.

That God was shocked at the effect of the flood is clear in that he made a decision never again to destroy mankind by flood waters. This became a covenant between God and Noah, and the rainbow became the sign of this pledge. (Genesis 9:12-17.) There are many who find themselves wondering if we are to believe that the rainbow came into existence at just that instant and that never before had the prismatic effect of the sunlight on the misty cloud been present in the sky. Such a limited interpretation will rob the student of the tremendous significance that although the rainbow had been there from the dawn of light and from the time when the mist rose from off the earth, it was Noah who interpreted it as the symbol of the covenant between God and himself, that never again would such an all-inclusive flood destroy man.

Liquor throughout the course of history has been a source of trouble. Noah planted a vineyard. (Genesis 9:20.) He drank of the wine and was drunk, and "was uncovered within his tent." (Genesis 9:21.) Nakedness was regarded as shameful even from the days of the Garden of Eden when Adam and Eve made clothes. In this instance, however, Ham, the youngest of Noah's sons, passed the tent and discovered his father's condition and relayed the information to Shem and Japheth, his brothers, who took a garment and went backward into their father's tent to cover him. When Noah awakened from his drunken stupor, he was furious, and pronounced a curse upon Canaan who was Ham's son, and upon all the children of Canaan on down through the years. Thus the curse instead of falling upon Ham, himself, was laid through these centuries upon Ham's descendants, the children, the grandchildren, and the millions yet unborn. While most of us think in terms of Adam as the father of the races, it was not Adam alone, for Adam's children with the exception of Noah and Noah's fam-

20

ily were wiped out at the time of the flood. The races trace their beginnings to Ham, Shem and Japheth.

Finally, we have one concluding fact about Noah. While Methuselah has the record for living to be the world's oldest man in that he attained the ripe majority of nine hundred and sixty-nine years (Genesis 5:27), it is to be observed that Noah ran him a close second, for at the time he died he had reached the incredible age of nine hundred and fifty years. (Genesis 9:29.)

Job

Time: *Sixth century* B.C.

Place: *Uz—thought to be in the same general vicinity of Ur of the Chaldees*

Scripture: *Book of Job*

In its composition the Book of Job is a poetical biography. This in no wise detracts from its forcefulness, and the fact is mentioned only because in certain versions the poetic translation does not appear. Compare the Revised Standard Version with the King James Version.

Actually, so far as its structure is concerned, one could say that it is a religious drama in which there are scenes on earth and scenes in heaven, where there are entrances and exits; yet its import is that of a philosophical forum in which the great question "Why does a good man suffer?" is tossed back and forth and is argued pro and con.

Scene I (Job 1:1-5) gives the setting. Job, a man of great wealth whose family is large and whose manner is gracious, is pictured living in the land of Uz.

Scene II (Job 1:6-12) shifts to heaven where "the sons of God came to present themselves before the LORD, and Satan came also among them." There is something very impertinent in the attitude of Satan. The LORD says, "Whence have you come?" To which Satan makes reply, "From going to and fro on the earth, and from walking up and down on it." The LORD then asks if Satan has noticed Job, to which Satan answers that he has noticed that Job is a God-fearing person, but why would he not reverence the LORD since he has prospered him so abundantly. Then to the reader's dismay, the LORD turns Job over to Satan to do with as he will, "Only upon himself do not put forth your hand."

Scene III (Job 1:13-22) shows the immediate action that Satan brings upon Job. First, report comes that all of the oxen and the asses have been stolen by the Sabeans. Second, word comes that lightning has killed the sheep. Third, a messenger stumbles in with the news that the Chaldeans have made a raid upon the camels. Lastly, the tragic word comes that Job's sons and daughters have been killed.

Job arises, tears his clothes to shreds, shaves his head, and falls down upon the ground to lament, "Naked I came from my mother's womb, and naked shall I return; the LORD gave, and the LORD has taken away, blessed be the name of the LORD."

"In all this Job did not sin, or charge God with wrong."

Scene IV (Job 2:1-6) returns to heaven. Again the LORD asks Satan: "Whence have you come?" And again the reply, "From going to and fro on the earth, and from walking up and down on it." The LORD is rather proud of Job, but Satan says that while the losses have come, actually he has suffered no physical pain. Then the LORD turns Job over to Satan with the reservation, "only spare his life."

Scene V, which embraces the rest of the book, takes place entirely upon earth. Satan wastes no time but proceeds immediately to afflict Job with sores from the soles of his feet to the crown of his head. This must have been painful, and the agony of the poor man is at its peak when he takes a piece of broken pottery and scrapes the sores, then gathers a little batch of ashes and sits in them.

Job's wife comes to him at this point and suggests that he defy God. "Curse God, and die." "But he said to her, 'You speak as one of the foolish women would speak. Shall we receive good at the hand of God, and shall we not receive evil?' In all this Job did not sin with his lips."

Hearing of his distress, three friends, Eliphaz the Temanite, Bildad the Shuhite, and Zophar the Naamathite, make "an appointment together to come to condole with him and comfort him." (Job 2:11c.)

The disfigurement of the sores is so great, however, that they do not even recognize him. For seven days and seven nights they sit in silence. Then follow three cycles of speeches.

Job begins with the outcry:

"Let the day perish wherein I was born,
    and the night which said,
      'A man-child is conceived.' " (3:3)

He believes that if he had never been born, he would never have suffered.

"Why is light given to him that is in misery,
    and life to the bitter in soul?" (3:20)

Eliphaz begins courteously enough.

"If one ventures a word with you, will you be offended?"
    (4:2)

But he immediately starts accusing Job of dire sin.

"who that was innocent ever perished? . . .
. . . those who plow iniquity
    and sow trouble reap the same." (4:7-8)

In a long paragraph he tries to establish the premise that God is always right, hence Job has to be in the wrong.

Job's quaint wit comes out clearly in his reply.

"Does the wild ass bray when he has grass,
    or the ox low over his fodder?" (6:5)

He is hurt and he tries to make his friends see that he himself has not sinned. They must accept his innocence before they can comfort him.

Bildad becomes sarcastic.

"How long will you say these things,
    and the words of your mouth be a great wind?
Does God pervert justice?" (8:2)

24

He intimates that Job has hidden his sin.

"If you will seek God . . .

. . . surely then he will rouse himself for you." (8:5-6)

Job asks searchingly,

". . . how can a man be just before God?" (9:2b)

He goes on to say that God is overwhelmingly big.

"If it is a contest of strength, behold him!

. . . .

For he is not a man, as I am, that I might answer him,
    that we should come to trial together.

There is no umpire between us,
    who might lay his hand upon us both." (9:19a, 32-33)

Zophar does not agree.

"Should a multitude of words go unanswered . . .?

For you say, 'My doctrine is pure,
    and I am clean in God's eyes.' " (11:2, 4)

He wishes that God would speak to discipline Job.

"Know . . . that God exacts of you less than your guilt deserves." (11:6c)

Job does not like this and he returns harsh words for harsh words.

"No doubt you are the people,
    and wisdom will die with you,

But I have understanding as well as you;
    I am not inferior to you. (12:2-3)

What you know, I also know; . . .
    and I desire to argue my case with God." (13:2a, 3b)

He knows that he is on dangerous grounds and he admits fearfully,

". . . he will slay me; I have no hope;
    yet I will defend my ways to his face." (13:15)

He raises the question,

"If a man die, shall he live again?" (14:14a)

25

Eliphaz derides Job.

"Should a wise man answer with windy knowledge,
    and fill himself with the east wind?

. . . .

Your own mouth condemns you and not I;
    your own lips testify against you." (15:2 and 6)

Eliphaz insists that righteousness and prosperity go hand in hand.

Job says,

"Miserable comforters are you all.

. . . .

God gives me up to the ungodly,
    and casts me into the hands of the wicked.

. . . .

Although there is no violence in my hands,
    and my prayer is pure." (16:2b, 11, 17)

Bildad has no patience with this position.

"How long will you hunt for words?" (18:2a)

Then he insists that terrors will come upon Job, for such is the situation of the wicked.

Job knows better than this.

"How long will you torment me,
    and break me in pieces with words?

. . . .

God has put me in the wrong,
    and closed his net about me.
Behold, I cry out, 'Violence!' but I am not answered." (19: 2, 6a-7a)

Then come the familiar words,

". . . . I have escaped by the skin of my teeth." (19: 20)

And the declaration:

"Oh that my words were written! . . .
Oh that with an iron pen and lead
    they were graven in the rock for ever!

26

For I know that my Redeemer lives,
        and at last he will stand upon the earth;
and after my skin has been thus destroyed,
        then without my flesh shall I see God." (19:23a, 24-
        26)

Following this speech there is yet one more cycle of the speeches. The three friends persist in saying that Job is wrong, that he has sinned, that he must have done something dreadful or he would be well and rich. Job's final speech runs from chapter 26 through chapter 31. He vouches for the fact that he has lived uprightly, describes his ways of dealing with the poor, the needy, the unfortunate.

A young philosopher by the name of Elihu speaks for untried youth. His words lack the pungency of the other speeches.

In conclusion God comes onto the scene. He requires Eliphaz and Zophar to bring seven bulls and seven rams to offer as a burnt sacrifice. He demands that they shall entreat Job to pray for them. Wealth is bestowed upon Job. He is blessed with seven new sons and three daughters. "And Job died, an old man, and full of days." (42:17)

Abraham

Father: *Terah*

Mother: *Not known*

Place: *Ur of the Chaldeans, Haran, Canaan, Egypt*

Scripture: *Genesis 11:27—25:10; Isaiah 41:8, 51:2; John 8:33; Acts 7:2; Romans 4; Galatians 3:6—4:31; Hebrews 11:8-10; James 2:21*

Abram, respected by the Jews, by the Christians, and by the Mohammedans, stands as one of the great religious figures of all time.

The Jews claim him because they say that they are Abraham's children through Isaac and Jacob, and they cherish the covenant (Genesis 17:2) which God made with Abraham at the time that Isaac was promised.

The Mohammedans claim him through Ishmael who was the son of Hagar, the unwed wife of Abraham.

As for the Christians, we respect Abraham as a man of surpassing faith and accept him because he is inseparably linked with Christian teachings in the New Testament. See Romans 4 and Hebrews 11:8-10.

Abram's name originally meant "the father is high," but this was changed years later to Abraham which carried the meaning of "father of a great multitude." (Genesis 17:5.) He came from Ur of the Chaldeans, which was that part of the Arabian desert to the far east on the banks of the Euphrates River. There the call had come to his father, Terah, to leave and to move westward, so Terah moved to the uppermost tip of the crescent and there sickened, whereupon the pilgrimage was halted until his death. Then Abram continued the journey into this "promised land."

It must have been a disappointing experience to get to Canaan only to find it a barren waste. Abram moved on south into Egypt to get food with which to sustain his own life and the lives of his cattle and camels.

When Abram got to Egypt, he told Sarah, his wife, that she was so very beautiful that she would have to pretend to be his sister and to allow the Pharaohs to have her for their harem. He was sure that he would be killed if it were known that she was his wife. (Genesis 12:12.) To all intents and purposes Abraham profited wonderfully by the transaction, for when the Pharaohs found out that she was married to Abram, they paid him off liberally, but asked that he take Sarah and leave their domain forever. (Genesis 12:20.)

Had Abram done this only once it would have been understood as a virtual necessity, but when he arranged for a similar guising of Sarah as his sister to Abimelech, upon his return to Palestine, it becomes perfectly clear that in his thinking there was nothing particularly amiss in such misrepresentation as a sort of business technique. (Genesis 20:1-12.) Through a technicality she was his half sister, for the text says that she and Abraham had the same father but different mothers. (Genesis 20:12.) Apparently their relationship as man and wife was not extraordinary.

Frequently a man's character comes into focus through his dealings with others. Such is true in the case of Abraham and Lot, his nephew. There are three distinct stories of the dealings between these two, and each of them is unforgettable:

1. *Abram's Generosity with Lot* (Genesis 13:5-13): This is the story that most frequently goes under the caption of "Lot's Choice," for in the account the old man gave preferment to the younger; it was Lot's decision to go into the valley of Sodom and Gomorrah—those two cities that have been recognized as cities of unparalleled wickedness. Here it was that Abram, who

29

stands head and shoulders above his kind and above us as we would act in similar circumstances, gave away the rich and lush bottom land to the younger man.

2. *Lot's Capture by Chedorlaomer* (Genesis, chapter 14): This is a story of tremendous importance, not because of the kidnaping involved, although that is interesting, but because of the fact that upon returning from the engagement, Abram met with Melchizedek who bestowed God's blessing on Abram and whom we have come to know as one of the greatest of all priests. Abram's military tactics enabled him to recapture Lot and all of his family, without the loss of a single member of Abram's own forces.

3. *Rescue of Lot from Sodom and Gomorrah* (Genesis 18: 16-29): This was brought about as the result of the appeal of Abraham, who tried to save the two cities. If only ten righteous men could have been found there, the cities could have been preserved, but the very measure of their own evil was hopeless.

That Abraham should have had two wives, Hagar and Sarah, is not surprising, but Sarah's jealousy of Hagar because she was able to bear Abraham a son, Ishmael, and the fact that he and his mother should have been driven out into the desert to die of thirst, border upon criminality. Yet it is through Ishmael that the Arabians trace their connection with Abraham. Compare Genesis, chapter 16, with Genesis 21:9-21. One story has it that it was at the time of Hagar's pregnancy that Abraham drove her away into the desert. The other story has it that little Isaac, whose name means "laughter," was playing with this older boy, Ishmael, and that Sarah, fearing that Ishmael might become an heir with her son, demanded that Abraham drive Hagar and Ishmael away.

The covenant relationship with God began to take focus with Abraham. Although a covenant had been made with Noah, that the earth would never again be destroyed by water (Genesis 9:16-17), it was with Abraham that several other things were set apart as religious practices, and as parts of the God-with-man agreement. One is the rite of circumcision (Genesis 17:10) which was practiced upon both Ishmael and Isaac. This practice, through the long centuries, has been for the Jews a religious necessity, for the non-Jews a hygienic advantage. It became a stumbling block for the early Christians because of those who insisted that all Christians had to be circumcised. It was Paul, the great apostle to the Gentiles, who helped make it clear that, from the Christian point of view, circumcision was not a necessity. (Colossians 3:11 and Galatians 6:15.)

Another covenant relationship is the matter of the tithe which came into its beginning with Abraham's paying to Melchizedek one tenth of all he had. (Genesis 14:20.) It is to be remembered that this was a mark of Abraham's faith, a part of his worship, and the key to his own great blessing from God.

That Abraham should have been able to break with the custom of human sacrifice, which was the practice of those tribes in and around him, becomes a monument of blessing, because that needless waste of human life has left its mark all over the world. There is no doubt that the temptation to offer Isaac as a human sacrifice was strong. It would have left an indelible impression of Abraham's love for his God, but how much finer it was that Abraham saw that God did not want human sacrifice and for that reason spared Isaac. (Genesis 22:1-14.) Had not Abraham had the experience with Isaac on the mountain, and had he not seen that it was possible to substitute a ram in the place of the son, it is entirely possible that human sacrifice would have become an accepted part of the faith of the Jews, the Christians, and the Mohammedans.

Abraham's purchase of the cave of Machpelah from the Hittites is one of the classical stories of the Old Testament. (Genesis 23:3-20.) The suave politeness of the Oriental chieftain, the apparent generosity that became a veneer for the business of buying and selling, the apparent contempt for the purchase price of a field—that purchase price being probably ten times what the field was worth—are excellent examples of the gra-

31

cious business transactions of biblical history. The fact remains, however, that it was a binding contract, and that it held through the long generations that were to follow, and that the dead who were placed therein were never rudely disturbed.

At long last, the time came for Abraham to die. He was 175 years of age. (Genesis 25:7-8.) And in the same cave of Machpelah where Sarah lay buried, his sons put Abraham.

Isaac

Father: *Abraham*

Mother: *Sarah*

Scripture: *Genesis 15:4—35:29*

A tremendous emphasis is placed upon the fact that Isaac was born as one out of season; for Sarah, his mother, was well-nigh a feeble woman at the time she gave birth to the child. In fact the name "Isaac," which means laughter, is attributed to this circumstance. (Genesis 18:12.) The very thought of having a child at her time of life seemed utterly preposterous, hence her laughter.

While emphasis is generally placed upon Abraham's faith in the story of his taking of his son Isaac up onto Mount Moriah (Genesis, chapter 22), the matter of Isaac's training of complete obedience to his father seems to have been relatively unnoticed. The scholars point out that Isaac was no child but rather was a full-grown youth, and that to overpower his aged father should have been a relatively easy matter. The reason for going along with Abraham, for submitting when his father actually tied him upon the altar, of being acquiescent before what he realized was sure death for him, indicates that any thought of rebellion against his father's authority was nonexistent.

This same note of complete parental jurisdiction seems to dominate the story of the purchase of a wife for Isaac who was forty years of age at the time. An arrangement was made that was completely satisfactory so far as its financial expectations were concerned. All parties seemed satisfied with the transaction, and Rebekah was taken back to Palestine to become the bride of Isaac.

Isaac stayed in the background through the unfolding of all these events until he became feeble and blind. He knew that death was not too far off for him, and he asked his elder son, Esau, who was the huntsman, to kill a deer and to prepare the meat and bring it to him for he wished to give him a parental blessing. (Genesis, chapter 27.) The story reveals several things to us, namely the simple honesty of Isaac, the cunning of Rebekah, the trickery of Jacob, and the wholesome manliness and uprightness of Esau. Jacob deceived Isaac. He put sheepskin on his forearms and on the nape of his neck, and permitted his aged father to pour out upon him the blessing that the father intended for Esau.

Isaac died at Mamre at the remarkable age of one hundred and eighty years. His sons Esau and Jacob buried him. (Genesis 35:28-29.)

Rebekah

Father: *Bethuel*

Mother   *Not known*

Place: *Mesopotamia, Haran, Palestine*

Scripture: *Genesis 24:15—49:31; Romans 9:10*

A study of Rebekah shows us a woman who had been trained to work, as had indeed all the women of her time, for she was a carrier of water. (Genesis 24:16.) But that she should offer to give water to a stranger and offer to water his animals was "like going the second mile" as in Jesus' teaching.

There was no hesitancy on the part of Rebekah when she was being sold by her brother. (Genesis 24:53.) She lived in an age when women were sold in marriage and they had a certain source of pride in bringing a good price. And then there was a spirit of adventure in going west where her father had told her that the others had gone!

The children that Rebekah bore to Isaac were as different as two boys well might be. One was red and hairy and was called "Hairy," for "Esau" means just that. The other was called "Jacob" which means "supplanter." The natures of the two boys were as different as those of Cain and Abel, and it was only by the speedy escape of Jacob that murder was avoided in this instance, for Esau doubtless would have killed Jacob. (Genesis 27:41-42.)

As parents Isaac and Rebekah had their favorites. Isaac was partial to Esau, the out-of-door man, the hunter. He

35

wanted to bless him, for not only was he the first-born but he was the manly sort, the open-faced, honest type. Jacob, on the other hand, seems to have had Rebekah's face.

It shocks us to realize that although Rebekah was partial to Jacob, she taught him to deceive his father. That the boy's mother should have urged him to such practices is unthinkable to us, according to Christian standards as we know them. But very evidently she felt it was quite all right for her to get for her boy the blessing of the father.

Never was any woman more in error, however, than Rebekah when she said, "Upon me be your curse, my son." (Genesis 27:13.) Little did she realize that evil brings its own punishment. Was it she who had to flee from Esau? Was it she who bore the sorrow when Joseph was sold into slavery while Jacob himself was told that the child was dead? (Genesis 37:31-34.) No, Rebekah's counsel was evil and her own son bore the brunt of it.

Because the main course of the Scripture deals with Jacob and because Jacob left home to make his way with Laban, our actual acquaintance with Rebekah ends with her farewell to Jacob. There is no mention in the text as to the death of Rebekah. We know only that she was buried in the cave of Machpelah where Abraham and Sarah were and where Isaac had been laid. (Genesis 49:31.)

Esau

Father: *Isaac*

Mother: *Rebekah*

Place: *Palestine, and the Arabian Desert*

Scripture: *Genesis 25:24—36:43; Deuteronomy 2:1-8, 26-37*

Esau, Jacob's twin, was called the "hairy" one. As he grew through boyhood, he came to be interested in the out-of-door things. He was a hunter and a lover of the manly arts. This pleased his father; it should have pleased his mother, too, but was of no interest to her because she was not fond of him and preferred his brother Jacob. (Genesis 25:24-29.)

The fact that he was the first-born, although a twin, would mean that he had the rights of inheritance. This means very little to the average American, because the first-born shares with the other sons and daughters in the family; but in the desert countries and in England it is the first-born who succeeds to the inheritance, gets all the property, and enjoys all the benefits of the accumulated wealth. This was not a thing for which he had to work—it was his as his birthright.

Jacob was a good cook, and one day when Esau came in from the field from his hunting hungry, he found that Jacob had cooked some pottage. He asked for a meal. Jacob declared he would sell his food for Esau's birthright. Much comment has been made on the fact that Esau traded this right of inheritance, and the Scripture specifically says that he "despised his birthright"; yet if he was as faint as he appears

37

to have been, and if it was a matter of life or death, then it may have been that Esau had a case. (Genesis 25:30-34.)

One of the laws of life among those tribal people was the matter of obedience to the patriarch, the old man of the tribe. When Isaac asked Esau to get him some venison, there was no hesitation. (Genesis 27:1-5.) Esau went to seek it. He practiced no deceit. He did not get a goat or lamb and spice it up, and "say" that it was venison. He went out to the hunt and got the venison, and brought it to his father. Then he discovered that he had been cheated. (Genesis 27:30-40.) Jacob had come with highly spiced food and had deceived the blind old father and received the blessing. There must have been keen disappointment when Esau realized that not only his birthright was gone from him, but now the blessing from his father had been taken from him, and he pleaded with his father for "one blessing," then lifted up his voice and wept. Isaac then told Esau that he would live by the sword. (Genesis 27:38-40.)

Esau, who had no deceit in his make-up and who through every account that is given proved himself to be the model of honesty and uprightness, threatened the life of Jacob. Rebekah, his mother, spirited Jacob away by night, and sent him to Laban, her brother, to get a wife. By the very fact that Jacob was gone, the matter rested and no harm was done. (Genesis 27:41-46.)

Jacob's absence from Esau seems to have covered twenty years—seven years that he worked to pay for Leah, seven that he worked to pay for Rachel, and six years that he worked to buy Laban's cattle. It is entirely possible that Esau could have nursed his grudge against Jacob, could have kept a smoldering hatred for him, but such seems not to have been the case. The old proverb that the "wicked flee when none pursue" seems to have been proved in this experience, for Esau never went after Jacob to do him harm, yet Jacob carried in his heart all those twenty years the wrong that he had done to Esau and to Isaac. As Jacob was returning, he sent advance word to Esau that he was coming back to Canaan. Then the news reached him that Esau was coming to meet him with four hundred horsemen.

Jacob was thoroughly scared. It could be that Esau would come to fight, and would seize this opportunity to avenge the ancient wrong. Jacob sent forward at well-spaced intervals great gifts of cattle and sheep—presents that were tremendous in their value. These became installments of a kind. Jacob hoped to assuage the possible anger of Esau. Then Jacob divided his family into groups. First went forward the hand-maidens and their children, then Leah and her sons, and lastly Rachel, who was throughout Jacob's life the one he loved supremely.

Esau magnanimously forgave the whole business, declared that he rejoiced at seeing Jacob, welcomed him, and refused the thought of such magnificent gifts as the three groups of cattle and sheep. (Genesis 33:9.) Jacob was tremendously relieved, but insisted that Esau must accept the gifts (Genesis 33:11), and so the two men were reconciled. All of this was made possible only because of Esau's graciousness.

In that general area to the east and south of the Dead Sea is a large area known as Edom. It is to this general area that Esau eventually migrated (Genesis 36:6-8) because the brothers had such enormous herds of cattle and sheep that there was not room for both in the land of Canaan. There Esau established himself and became the father of the Edomites. Through the years the separation from Jacob became more and more fixed in the thinking of the families and the tribes, as they must rightly be considered.

Just when Esau died, the text does not say. It was only when the children of Israel returned from Egypt after the long years of their bondage that they were told they were not to attack the Edomites, for they were the descendants of Esau and, as such, they bore the protection of God. (Deuteronomy 2:4-8.)

Jacob (Israel)

Father: *Isaac*

Mother: *Rebekah*

Place: *Palestine*

Scripture: *Genesis 25:24—50:14*

Jacob was born after his twin Esau. It is reported that the hand of Jacob held onto the heel of his brother at the time of birth, and from this circumstance he was given the name of Jacob which means "supplanter." (Genesis 25:26.) Throughout his days he was forever seeking advantage and was pressing it at every hand.

The natures of the twins differed. Esau was an outdoor man, for he liked to hunt, whereas Jacob was a quiet man dwelling in tents. (Genesis 25:27.) It is interesting, too, that the Scripture specifically mentions the fact that the boy Jacob was his mother's favorite, while Esau was the father's.

That Jacob should have been willing to take advantage of his brother's being near the point of starvation, and insisting that Esau must sell his birthright, has been a source of endless discussion. The emphasis has always been upon the theory that Esau despised his birthright and seemingly few words have been presented to the effect that Jacob's attitude was one of greed and utterly lacking in what we today would call common hospitality and the milk of human kindness. (Genesis 25:29-34.)

When Rebekah persuaded Jacob to deceive his old and blind father, the youth instinctively revolted at the idea. It may have been that he was fearful lest he be caught in the deception and that the fear of being caught worried him more than the moral implications involved. (Genesis 27:11.) To say the least, the record points clearly to the fact that Rebekah urged the business and insisted upon its prosecution. She declared to Jacob that if any harm came, she would want to bear the guilt of it. (Genesis 27:13.) What she overlooked was the fact that no mother can bear the curse for the sins that her son commits. Each man has to bear the stripes of his own evil. Jacob literally had to flee for his life. (Genesis 27:42.)

That Jacob should have gone to Haran is perfectly natural. It was from Haran that his mother had come, and she would urge him to return to her people and to the household of her brother.

The vision of the ladder when he slept at Bethel, was the paramount religious experience of Jacob's life. Certainly he regarded it as a covenanting occasion between himself and God, for it was then he agreed that henceforth he would pay the tithe. This would mean that one tenth of all that came to him would be paid to the work of the LORD. (Genesis 28:22.)

As soon as Jacob reached Haran, he met Rachel and the love between these two became one of the sweetest love stories of all time. He seems to have been smitten from the very first—a case of love at first sight.

The moral of Jacob's life is almost too clearly defined to miss. That he should have gone before his blind father wearing sheepskin on his arms and on the back of his neck seemed bad enough, yet in the course of the years there came a time when he, himself, was deceived; for not only did he have to pay sadly for that wrong, but he had to pay double. In the first instance there was the time when he was deceived by Laban. Jacob had no means, and he lived in a time when it was the custom to buy one's wife. Since he had no money with which to pay for her, Jacob offered the tremendous price of seven years of labor for Rachel. This must have been a goodly sum according to the times, and indicates how great was his love for her. Then on the wedding night Laban put him into the tent with Leah instead of with Rachel, and then insisted that he must work another seven years for Rachel. (Genesis 29: 25.) This must have been a rather trying matter for him and maybe he remembered that he had deceived his old blind father years before.

What constituted a flight of the first order from the reaches of Laban was the thing that brought about the giving of the Mizpah which, within certain limits, originally meant a threat. Laban overtook the fleeing Jacob and all his cattle and his possessions, as well as his men servants and maid servants, at Mizpah, and there it was agreed that neither would cross the line thereafter. Laban assured Jacob that if he harmed Rachel or Leah, he would seek him out and no man would be able to stop what he would do to him. (Genesis 31:43-55.)

Jacob's wrestling with the messenger of God at Peniel (Genesis 32:24-32) comes down to us as the reason for his decided limp, and for the fact that his name was changed from "the supplanter" to "Prince of God" which is the meaning of the name "Israel." The fact that this occurred when Jacob was en route to meet Esau is particularly interesting due to the fact that he had so long been estranged, and due to the fact that he was in mortal fear lest Esau should bear the grudge from the wrong of years before, and Jacob sorely needed the help of the LORD at that particular time.

Then, too, there was the instance where, as he himself grew old, Jacob made a long robe with sleeves for his favorite son, Joseph. Joseph was stripped of his robe by his brothers and thrown into a pit. When the robe was brought to Jacob torn to shreds and covered with blood and dirt, he supposed that Joseph was dead. He did not suppose for a moment that the youth had been sold into slavery by his brothers. Such was the family situation with Jacob's sons. (Genesis 37:29.) Again it might be cause for wonder if he recalled the time when he had deceived his own father years before.

Jacob went to Egypt ignorant of the fact that Joseph was second only to the throne. There is nothing in Jacob's life more picturesque or more real than his presentation before Pharaoh. The Scripture tells it magnificently, and one can fairly see Joseph, the wise, the discreet counselor and the favored one, bringing his aged father before the ruler. Out of courtesy the Pharaoh allowed him to come into his very presence, and the aged Jacob proceeded to give a blessing to the ruler. Then Pharaoh asked the patriarch how old he was, and talked to him as kindly as he could, and when the interview was over, Jacob again gave a blessing upon Pharaoh and went out. (Genesis 47:7-10.) Later Joseph brought his sons, Ephraim and Manasseh, to have the aged Jacob give his benediction upon the boys. This the old man did, giving preferment to Ephraim, the younger, by putting his right hand upon his head. This Joseph sought to correct, but Jacob would have none of it, and declared that the younger son should be the preferred one. (Genesis 48:15-22.)

Whenever one speaks of the twelve sons of Jacob, one thinks of the twelve tribes of Israel—and certainly that should be borne in mind—yet for all that, it is not absolutely right. Levi was one of the sons of Jacob whose other name was Israel, and the tribe of Levi was one of the tribes; but when the land of Canaan was divided into twelve parts, Levi did not inherit a part, because that tribe was of the priestly line and lived upon the tithe. The other tribe that did not inherit was the tribe of Joseph. Joseph's two sons, Ephraim and Manasseh, inherited for these two. Thus there were actually thirteen tribes of Israel—twelve that inherited land and one that was the priestly tribe. Study Genesis 48:20.

The order in which the sons were born follows:

Leah bore:

Reuben	(1)—Genesis 29:32
Simeon	(2)—Genesis 29:33
Levi	(3)—Genesis 29:34
Judah	(4)—Genesis 29:35
Issachar	(9)—Genesis 30:18
Zebulun	(10)—Genesis 30:20

Zilpah, who was the handmaid of Leah, bore Jacob the following sons:

Gad	(7)—Genesis 30:11
Asher	(8)—Genesis 30:13

Bilhah, who was the handmaid of Rachel, bore Jacob the following sons:

Dan	(5)—Genesis 30: 6
Naphtali	(6)—Genesis 30: 8

Rachel, who was his favorite, bore two:

Joseph	(11)—Genesis 30:24
Benjamin	(12)—Genesis 35:16

Pharaoh was generous with Joseph, and when his father died, Joseph was allowed a company of chariots and horsemen to take the remains back to the cave of Machpelah. Jacob's body was embalmed (Genesis 50:13), and a ceremony that lasted a number of weeks took place before the final mourning was at its end. He was laid to rest beside Leah as mentioned specifically in his request.

Joseph

Father: *Jacob*

Mother: *Rachel*

Place: *Canaan and Egypt*

Scripture: *Genesis 30:22—50:26*

Joseph has long been called the most Christlike character of the Old Testament. In circumstances that seem to have run the complete gamut of the experiences to which the flesh is heir, Joseph conducted himself most decorously. At no time did he return evil for evil. At no time did he despise his condition or curse those who used him unjustly.

He was the first-born son of Rachel and as such he was the favorite of his father, Jacob. It was for Joseph that a special long robe with sleeves was made; and it was this mark of special favoritism that brought the jealousy of his half-brothers upon him. They despised the robe because it symbolized for them that Joseph was favored over them.

This, added to the fact that Joseph had the unhappy faculty of telling about his various dreams, boded him no good. The dream of the sheaves (Genesis 37:5-8) and the one of the sun, moon, and the eleven stars (Genesis 37:9-11) had a common message. In each, Joseph was the favored one, and to all intents and purposes even his father and mother were made to bow before him and his work. This was too much for the brothers, who seized the chance to capture him when he came to learn of their place of pasturage.

The brothers were ready to slay him and were kept from their purpose only by the intervention of Reuben who suggested that they should not kill him but put him in a pit, and by Judah who proposed that they should sell him to the passing caravan of Midianites.

The moral stamina of Joseph certainly was of the highest order. His exemplary conduct in the temptation that he faced with Potiphar's wife is one of the finest examples we have of a man's virtuous living. The fact that the woman used every known artifice to ensnare the young Hebrew is taken for granted. What is probably as true as human nature itself, is the fact that a woman scorned and spurned is not a very agreeable creature. Her false accusation against the young slave brought immediate action, and Joseph was thrown into prison for being virtuous, for having respect for his master's wife, and for obeying the teachings of his father. (Genesis, chapter 39.)

That this lad with a prison record, actually in the clothes of the jail, should ever have been raised from the position of non-entity and slavery to the place second only to the Pharaoh himself is, indeed, the handiwork of God. It was as interpreter of dreams that the wonderful advance was made. In that day a dream was looked upon as having tremendous meaning, as seeking by its symbolism to give to the dreamer a message that was for his own good, and which foretold coming events and conditions. The king's butler and the king's baker were thrown into the jail where Joseph was especially favored, and where he had been given practically the run of the place. Joseph came to know them both during the course of the time that they were awaiting a trial before Pharaoh. They dreamed dreams, which Joseph interpreted for them, and the interpretation came out as Joseph foretold—the baker was hanged, the butler restored. Unfortunately the chief butler forgot all about Joseph once he was himself restored. (Genesis, chapter 40.)

It is out of the remembrance of this experience, however, that Joseph's great opportunity came, for the Pharaoh had a dream of seven fat cows and seven lean cows which neither he nor his interpreters could understand or explain. It was then that the butler recalled his acquaintance with Joseph, and Joseph was called to the Pharaoh immediately. After Joseph interpreted the dream as seven years of plenty followed by seven years of famine, he was appointed by Pharaoh to oversee the whole land of Egypt. He was to arrange for storage of crops to bridge the seven lean years that the interpretation of the dreams indicated were sure to come. Undoubtedly God was using this young man for a mighty purpose. (Genesis, chapter 41.)

His brothers arrived from Canaan where the drought had struck hard. He could easily have made life difficult for them. And he did tease them just a little. He insisted that they bring Benjamin when next they should come, and he insisted that they had stolen some of his silver. It was all most confusing for the brothers, and certainly they deserved to worry just a little because they had played a scurvy trick on Joseph in selling him into slavery and in deceiving their aged father. Yet in due course Joseph forgave them all and blessed them with wealth and plenty. (Genesis, chapters 42—45.) Of course the climax came when they learned who he was and their amazement that he did not intend to punish them for what they had done to him was unbounded.

Joseph's wisdom in bringing the family to Egypt is questionable. It was when they moved to Egypt that they became dependent and sank into slavery. For hundreds of years they remained in that condition until Moses led them out by the grace and power of God.

It is interesting to note that Joseph married Asenath, the daughter of a priest of On. (Genesis 41:45.) She bore him two sons, Manasseh and Ephraim. (Genesis 41:51-52.) These sons later became heads of two tribes of Israel, for one took the place of the tribe of Levi in the inheritance, and the other the tribe of Joseph since no tribe bore his name. This rounds out the twelve tribes of Israel. That Jacob should have given his special blessing to Ephraim at the time the two boys were brought before him was a source of confusion to Joseph. He begged his father to give the special blessing to the first-born, Manasseh, but Jacob was determined and the blessing went primarily to Ephraim. (Genesis 48.)

When old age settled upon Joseph, instead of choosing to be buried in Egypt beside his wife and with his children, he asked to go up with the tribes when they went back to Canaan. (Genesis 50:24-26.) This was done. He was embalmed and put into a coffin. And in the course of the years the children of Israel actually took that coffin with them as Moses led them out of Egypt, and Joseph was buried in the cave of Machpelah. (Compare Exodus 13:19 and Joshua 24:32.)

Moses

Father: *Amram*

Mother: *Jochebed*

Place: *Egypt and Sinai Peninsula*

Scripture: *Exodus 2:1—Deuteronomy 34:12*

The name "Moses" means "to draw" (Exodus 2:10) and comes from the fact that Pharaoh's daughter drew the child out of the water. That such a story could have been told in ten verses is a marvel of writing. Incidentally, in the story no mention is made of the names of the mother or the father or the sister of the child, or of the Egyptian princess. The text never reveals the name of the princess, but the names of Moses' parents are made clear in Exodus 6:20 where we are told that his father's name was Amram and that his mother's name was Jochebed. The name of Miriam is given in Exodus 15:20.

The life of Moses is divided into three parts.

The First Period

The first part is covered completely in Exodus, chapter 2. There appear the stories of his birth, of his being taken into the household of the Pharaoh where he was reared with all the cultural and educational advantages of the court of Egypt. His tremendous sympathy with the oppressed Hebrew people carried him to the extreme action in which he killed one of the Egyptian taskmasters, who was observed in the routine business of beating a Hebrew slave.

The next day Moses observed two Hebrews fighting. It must have been disconcerting to Moses to see this. He had meant only to befriend them. It was well-nigh unthinkable to him that they should be at enmity with one another. Their insolent reply (Exodus 2:14) to the effect that they supposed he would kill them as he had the Egyptian on the day before, must have shocked him tremendously. In panic for his personal safety, and completely disillusioned in his idealism regarding his own people, Moses fled to Sinai where he married into the household of Reuel who was a priest of Midian.

The Second Period

For this second period of his life Moses lived the out-of-door existence of the desert people. He learned the way they told direction, the way they fought to protect themselves. It must have been during this period of his life that he learned self-mastery, developing a maturity of judgment that ripened into personal power. There was a magnetism about him, and a quality of command that gave him a sense of great self-assurance.

Moses had no thought of returning to Egypt. He knew that the Pharaoh who had known him and who had cared for him as he grew into manhood within the confines of the palace, was dead. (Exodus 2:23.) It came as a great surprise to him when he saw the burning bush and heard the voice speaking forth from it saying, ". . . put off your shoes from your feet, for the place on which you are standing is holy ground." (Exodus 3:5.)

Moses pleaded that he did not know why he should be selected to go to the Pharaoh to liberate the Hebrews from Egypt. God said that he would be with him. Moses replied that he did not know the name of God. God gave his name, "I AM WHO I AM." Moses claimed that the people would not believe him. God showed him the miracle of the rod and the serpent, and then of the leprous hand (Exodus 4:6), and finally of the water of the Nile becoming blood upon the dry land.

In spite of all this Moses still held back and claimed that he was no spokesman. Then God told him angrily that Aaron would go with him and be a mouthpiece for him.

At last Moses realized that he must go, and he took his departure from his father-in-law, Jethro, and went to Egypt.

The Third Period

That Moses should have been able to effect such a spiritual revival; that he should have been able to muster a group of leaders from among the submerged Hebrews, should have been able to organize them, and to persuade them to risk their lives for freedom, is a miracle. The slave mind does not respond too graciously or too wisely to the responsibilities that freedom brings. Truly the thing that Moses did for the people in leading them out under the hand of the LORD is as much of a miracle as anything could possibly be.

The first step in freeing the children of Israel was to bring about the ten plagues in the presence of Pharaoh. These were the plagues of blood, frogs, gnats, flies, diseases of cattle, boils, hail, locusts, darkness, and the destruction of the first-born. But Pharaoh's heart was hardened and he would not let the children of Israel leave until the tenth plague.

Among all the feasts that have been observed through the centuries, none seems to have left a more indelible impression upon the minds of people than the Passover of the Jews. It had its inception in the tenth of the plagues that came upon Egypt at the hand of Moses, and it was observed with the slaying of a lamb, and the spreading of the blood of a lamb over the lintel of the door. On that night the LORD passed over the homes of Egypt, and the first-born of every home was slain even to the household of the Pharaoh.

That night the Pharaoh gave his consent for Moses to take the children of Israel out of Egypt, and they fled with all their household goods and with everything they could carry away. The people had no time for the leaven to rise for the baking of bread

51

and they baked unleavened bread, which was nothing more than flour and water, and carried it with them. That was the origin of the matzoth which are used in Jewish observance of the Passover to this day, and of the "bread" on the communion tray of Christian churches.

The Lord on the night in which he was betrayed in Jerusalem was observing the Passover feast. (Read Matthew 26:26 ff. and compare it with Exodus 13:6 ff.)

Another comparison of great significance is the parallel between the paschal lamb which was slain and the fact that Jesus represents in Christian theology the Lamb of God who is to take away the sins of the world.

Unique as Moses is as a leader in almost every field of human relations, it is as a lawgiver that he stands at the peak. In his famous Ten Commandments, we have the foundational principles upon which Hebrew life and thought have been built through the centuries. (Exodus 20:3-17.)

Abbreviated they mean:

1. Worship God
2. Do not worship idols
3. Do not swear
4. Keep the Sabbath holy
5. Honor your parents
6. Do not kill
7. Do not commit adultery
8. Do not steal
9. Do not lie
10. Do not covet

(Embedded in the writing of Exodus 34 is what is called the ancient Code of Hammurabi. It is thought that this particular code was much more ancient than the one from Sinai. The Code is found in Exodus 34:14 ff.)

While it is a common thing to associate the Law with the Ten Commandments, this is really an error, because the Law was much more, and many times more, than the Ten Commandments. The Law covered all the petty matters of what to do with a child: its circumcision, the cleanliness of the mother, the matter of fevers and hygiene in general, the matters of stealing sheep, or of visitors who migrated from one camp to another. Practically all of the Book of Leviticus deals with the laws. In chapter 11 is the complete statement as to what food shall be eaten and what food shall not be eaten. Chapter 12 tells the matter of the purification of a woman after childbirth. Chapter 13 deals with the means of identifying leprosy.

The history of the wilderness experience is a chronicle of human frailty and of human advance. For the years of a complete new generation, these slaves lived in the great out-of-doors. It was unthinkable that a group of slave people should have been able to march into new territory to possess it. For generation upon generation they had been kept in subservience. The report of the spies shows a majority opinion. Of the twelve spies that went up to spy out the Promised Land only Caleb and Joshua returned with a promising prospect. All the others said that the project was unthinkable, they would be destroyed. They thought of themselves as grasshoppers. (Numbers, chapter 13.) Only one thing could happen if the whole of the Israelitish people were not to be destroyed, and that was for them to rear up a new generation who were freeborn and who were trained in the wild out-of-doors. That is what Moses did in biding his time. The oldsters died off. Those who had the slave-minds passed out of the picture, and it was the new generation who went up and possessed the land. The records bear out that there were some thirty-eight years that the tribes wandered in the territory north of Sinai.

Moses faced revolution and conquered it. (Numbers 16.) He faced heresy and he conquered it. (Numbers 21:7.) He faced organizational difficulties, and mastered them. (Exodus 18:17 ff.) He established a rule of orderly government. He insisted upon the sanctity of religion. In all these matters he was the unquestioned leader. The results of his work have been praised and appreciated in all succeeding generations.

Forewarned that his end was at hand (Numbers 27:12 ff.), Moses asked for a successor. The LORD named Joshua for this post. Then followed Moses' final preparation with the people. This is told in the Book of Deuteronomy. He made the appeal as a veritable revival. He recited for them their history, he went back into the giving of the great Law. He poured out for them his convictions upon the matter of their mission and their purpose. He outlined for them the possibilities of their success, and spurred them to action. Then after viewing the Promised Land which he himself was not privileged to enter, he died in the land of Moab. (Deuteronomy 34:5-6.) Few men have ever been more blessed or have ever lived a more useful life.

Aaron

Father: *Amram*

Mother: *Jochebed*

Places: *Egypt and Sinai Peninsula*

Scripture: *Exodus 4:14—Numbers 33:39*

Aaron is described in the very first mention of his name as
Aaron the Levite. It could quite as well have been said that
Moses was the Levite, for both of them were children of the
same father and mother and were full-bloodedly of the tribe of
Levi. Apparently it was Aaron who gave his whole talent to
the priestly office and to the priestly function, while Moses entered into the broader scope of political and social leadership.
Whereas Aaron was the man who carried the religious observances, who stood as the symbol of the priestly office, Moses was
the chief executive for the whole enterprise of the flight from
Egypt.

Aaron was a man of talent. He was a good spokesman (Exodus 4:14b) and there is every reason to believe that the two
brothers went into Egypt and preached a revival among the
people. For generations the worship of God had been neglected. The place and the power of religion had gone out of
the people's lives, and through these two men the voice of
God was heard in Egypt. There is every reason to believe that
Miriam organized the women quite as definitely as Aaron and
Moses organized the men. She was a leader and a singer of

very marked talent. She was a very definite force in the movement and she made a tremendous contribution to the success of the flight of the slave people from Egypt. (Exodus 15:20-21.)

Aaron seems not to have had the moral stamina of Moses. When Moses went up into Sinai and was gone for the forty days, Aaron listened to the voice of the people and allowed himself to be carried away with their enthusiasm for a reversion to the worship of the golden calf. (Exodus, chapter 32.)

From the very beginning the LORD decreed that there should be a place for the worship, there should be a religious center, and the tabernacle was to be that place. The art objects and the materials that were to be used in the ceremonies were to be kept there. Aaron was to be the keeper of this tabernacle, and his sons were to be the perpetuators of the worship program of the tribes. This tabernacle was filled with all manner of symbolic furnishings. There were to be the ark, the veil for the ark, the holy table, the lamp and the candlesticks, the golden vessels, and the laver. There were to be the uniforms that the priests would wear in performing their holy office. All of it was to be picturesque, and to the people who had been slaves in Egypt it was all magnificent and wonderful because it was their own.

(Leviticus 8 and 9.) The ceremony by which Aaron was installed as the head of the priestly line was picturesque and colorful, but the significance of what was done can scarcely be overestimated. Through all the long generations since then there has been this example to which the Hebrew children have looked back with respect. The tribe of Levi has had its sanction in the holy office from that original commitment. The keeping of the fire which came from the LORD (Leviticus 9:24) has been preserved even to this day as one of the most sacred privileges of the order.

Gradually the educational process evolved into the hands of these Levites. They became the teachers of the people in matters not only religious but educational, and while from time to time they fell into disrepute, the fact remains that they were wonderfully helpful in the setting of the religious and educational standards of the people. Again and again through the years there were prophets who cried for reform, and there were definite reforms accomplished, and the system continued, and the work of training the young was perpetuated.

In accordance with the LORD's command, Aaron was not permitted to go in the land of Edom. His garments were stripped from him and placed on his son Eleazar, who was to continue his priestly activities. Aaron died on the top of Mount Hor and the people wept for thirty days.

Joshua

Father: *Nun*

Mother: *Not known*

Place: *Egypt, Sinai Peninsula and Palestine*

Scripture: *Numbers 13—the Book of Joshua*

Joshua was the son of Nun and of the tribe of Ephraim. He seems to have had a sound knowledge of military science and tactics. At the time the Amalekites came up against Moses and the children of Israel when they were in the plain of Rephidim, Joshua was commissioned to lead the troops into the movement. It must have been with a realization that the hand of the Lord would have to be with them, that Joshua took his troops into this engagement. When Moses' hands were upheld, the battle seemed to go favorably for the Hebrews, and when his hands were lowered, the Amalekites seemed to prevail. Thus it was that Aaron and Hur had Moses sit down in order that they might continue to hold his hands aloft. Joshua and his troops prevailed.

When Moses was up on Mount Sinai when the Ten Commandments were given, Joshua was with him. (Exodus 32:17.) This would lead us to believe that Moses had great confidence in him, and that he counted heavily on his counsel.

At the time the spies were selected to go up into the Promised Land to search it out and to give their report on the probable success of an immediate invasion, Joshua insisted that the people would be able to subdue the land. There was no wavering in his own conviction that the Hebrews would be able to succeed under the leadership of God. They were furious at his report, however, and threatened to stone him and Caleb who acceded in the same opinion. (Numbers 14:6-10.)

It was out of this long acquaintance with the man, and out of complete confidence in his integrity and his ability, that Moses chose him to be his successor as the leader of the people. Moses realized that it would take a man of strong convictions, a man of principle, and a man who would know how to guide them through actual military danger. His selection proved to be a wise one.

It is not always the easiest assignment for a man to take up where another man has left off. Certainly it is many times difficult for a person to accomplish that which another has designed and dreamed. The plans for the invasion of Palestine had been in the process of formulation for years. The partitioning of the land had been agreed upon long before the actual invasion.

The LORD assured Joshua that he would be with him in the conquest of the land, and Joshua relayed this information to his generals, and the plans for the invasion were undertaken as a religious as well as a military strategy. (Joshua, chapters 1—4.)

There are few stories of history more thrilling than the story of the fall of Jericho beside the Jordan. Archeology supports the idea that the foundations of the walls were part stone and part wood, and builds upon the premise that these foundations were fired and that during the course of the six days of marching around the city, there was the constant firing of these foundations, with the result that the burning out of these wooden pieces brought about the total collapse of the superstructure of the walls on the seventh day.

There is little reason to suppose that Joshua had too much authority insofar as the group of the whole twelve tribes was concerned. Each seems to have carried on its own policies of warfare after the fall of Jericho. Joshua seems to have been obsessed with the idea of complete destruction of everything that was conquered. He seems to have been more afraid of the ideas of the conquered people than of anything else. He insisted at Ai that every living thing be killed, and that all the booty be totally destroyed. (There were to be no souvenir collectors in his army.) Not all the people followed his ideas, however, and the majority of the people seem to have infiltrated the land rather than actually conquering and possessing the country. His victories are recounted in Joshua, chapters 10 and 11. Actually the tribes were rather independent one of another with the result that they were a weak confederation. The history of the remaining period of the account in Joshua and the Judges seems to have been one of an effort to get the people to co-operate. Through this early part Joshua managed to maintain sufficient prestige as a leader and arbiter that he was heard in matters of boundary disputes and the like.

In the final settlement Joshua was granted the city of Timnathserah, where he lived until his death. It is interesting that this military leader became the spiritual guide in the concluding council that he called when he realized that his death was at hand. In the magnificent challenge to the Hebrews he said, "Choose this day whom you will serve, whether the gods your fathers served in the region beyond the River, or the gods of the Amorites in whose land you dwell; but as for me and my house, we will serve the LORD." (Joshua 24:30.)

Thus it was with a full heart and at the ripe age of one hundred and ten years that Joshua died.

Deborah

Father: *Not known*

Mother: *Not known*

Place: *Palestine*

Scripture: *Judges 4:4—5:31*

Among a people who through every generation have given their allegiance and respect to their masculine leaders, it is unique and decidedly out of the ordinary to find a woman as a judge of Israel. There were fifteen of these rulers, and Deborah stands as the lone feminine monarch among them.

Just how she came into power is a moot question. Out of what would seem to be common deduction comes the thought that this woman had tremendous ability in her own right, and came to be recognized as the leader of her people.

Her court was held under a palm tree, and seemingly people came from far and near to ask her aid in the settling of their problems.

Her prowess, however, seems to have been in the field of military science and tactics. The fact that the forces engaged in these tribal wars were small should not detract too much from the skill with which the victories were won. Sisera, who was the captain in charge of the tiny militia of one Jabin, a Canaanite king, had been giving a good deal of trouble to the Israelites who, although they "conquered" Canaan, were living pretty much in tents in mountain fastnesses. Just how extensive had been the trouble that Sisera had given to the Israelites is not stated. Very probably he made their lives rather miserable. He had chariots which were very useful in the flat country. He had trained soldiers who were able to fight on the plains.

Deborah called Barak to gather what volunteers he could and to make ready to destroy Sisera. He replied that he would not fight without her (Judges 4:8) but she assured him that while she was perfectly willing to go along, she was certain that the honors would go to a woman and not to him. This does not seem to have mattered to him too much. She let the word be known to Sisera that she and Barak were marshalling troops at Mount Tabor, and Sisera gathered a strong company of his men. Some nine hundred chariots of iron came out to do battle with the infiltrating Canaanites.

The plan worked. Deborah's men had the higher ground which was in itself an advantage. She had been able to lead Sisera to mountain territory for the actual fighting, and the result was that the chariots were useless and the men deserted them and fled afoot. (Judges 4:4-15.)

Jael, the wife of Heber, became, because of her daring, the heroine of the day by giving refuge to Sisera as he fled. He charged her to tell the enemy that he was not there, and to watch and to guard him. First she fed him milk which, added to his fatigue, made him so sleepy that he simply could not keep his eyes open. While he slept, she took a tent spike and drove it through his temple with a mallet. The arch enemy of Israel was slain. Jael had won the honors. (Judges 4:12-22.)

Then follows in Judges 5:2-31 what is known as Deborah's song. It seems to be in four parts:

1. Verses 2-5 praise the LORD, and tell of the terror of his approach.

2. Verses 6-11 describe the condition of Israel before Deborah's activity.

3. Verses 12-18 cite the gathering of the tribes of Israel to do battle.

4. Verses 19-31 tell of the victory of Israel and the death of Sisera.

As to the death of Deborah, there is no mention. Her work as judge seems to have been wise and sound, for the lone sentence appears: "And the land had rest for forty years."

Gideon

Father: *Joash*

Mother: *Not known*

Place: *Palestine in and about Jezreel, which was immediately west and south of the Sea of Galilee*

Scripture: *Judges 6:11—8:33*

The vulnerability of the children of Israel in their Promised Land was such that petty thievery thrived on every hand. Any man who possessed anything had to hide it from sight lest vandals come upon him and rob him of what little he might be able to raise or to harvest.

Gideon, the son of Joash the Abiezrite, was poor. He "beat out wheat in the wine press, to hide it from the Midianites," who seem to have been wandering through the land and stealing everything upon which they could lay their hands. Seeing the difficulty into which the people had fallen, the LORD decided to deliver his people, and to do it in such a way that the people would realize it had been done, not by their own cleverness or prowess, but by the hand of God. It was through Gideon that the deliverance was to be achieved.

Rather strangely Gideon protested that he was not a man of such ability or talent as the LORD might use. There is a ring to his words surprisingly reminiscent of the protests of Moses when the LORD called him. Gideon expostulated: "Pray, LORD, how can I deliver Israel? Behold, my clan is the weakest in Manasseh, and I am the least in my family." The LORD declared to him that all would go well and that Gideon would see the hand of the Lord in all that was done. This did not satisfy the fearful farmer. He insisted that he wanted to make an offering, and yet further, that he wanted and expected the Lord to show him a sign by which he would know that God intended these things. Thus it was that Gideon prepared a kid and unleavened cakes, and presented them before the angel of the Lord. These were put on a rock and were consumed by fire. Gideon was amazed and his faith was stirred.

Then an angel came to tell him to pull down the altar of Baal and the image of Asherah, and to build an altar to the Lord. So strong, however, were the devotees of Baal, that Gideon dared not destroy the grove by day lest he be seen. He took ten men, and they went to the grove by night and hewed the altar to the ground.

Surely enough the next day when the men of the city saw that the altar had been torn down, they were furious. They came to Joash and demanded that he give up his son, for they intended to kill him for the destruction of the altar. Very sagely, however, Joash asked them if they were followers of Baal or if they were followers of the Lord. If they were followers of Baal, was it possible that this so-called god was not able to fend for himself? The way in which Joash put the question persuaded the men, and they let Gideon alone.

Each of these two ventures having proved successful in his experiences in faith, Gideon decided to call the troops together to rid the country of the Midianites. In a most interesting way in trying to get specific answer to prayer, Gideon declared he would put a fleece of wool on the threshing floor, and if God was for him, it would be wet with dew, and all the earth floor would be dry. Then he would know that Israel would prosper in the fight. When it was so the next day, he called yet again upon the name of the Lord, and asked that the fleece should be dry and the earth wet. So it happened and Gideon prepared for battle. (Judges 6:36-40.)

That Gideon should have had another name comes as a surprise to many people, for the one name has been so popular. Nevertheless, the other name was Jerubbaal. The names differ, for Gideon means "one who cuts down," whereas the other means "let Baal plead."

Such strategy as this extraordinary leader used was entirely new to his day, and would likely be to our own. Of the 32,000 men all who were afraid were allowed to go home, all who were sluggish were culled, and only 300 were chosen for the demonstration that by God's strategy the battle could be won. The three hundred men surrounded the camp with trumpets in one hand and a torch in the other. The Midianites took it that each torch represented a veritable regiment of men, and they fled in wild disorder and were mowed down by the troops under Gideon.

Very easily Gideon could have marshalled the men under himself, and could have established a dynasty. The people came to him and urged him to do that very thing, "Rule over us, you, and your son and your grandson also; for you have delivered us out of the hand of Midian." Gideon, however, was far more interested in the welfare of the people than in his own advantage, and he said, "I will not rule over you, my son will not rule over you; the LORD will rule over you." (Judges 8: 22-23.)

He did receive tribute money from the people, however, and with it he cast images of gold which became a source of idol worship throughout the little territory over which he judged. (Judges 8:24-27.) In addition to this he had a veritable multitude of wives and concubines, and was the father of seventy sons.

When he died, his plans went for nothing. His household was neglected, and the prestige with which he had managed the affairs of Israel for forty years faded and ceased to exist.

To this day, the name of Gideon is like magic. There are men who love the very sound of it. There is a society which places the Bible in hotels and motels as an instrument of conversion. They call themselves the Gideons. They hark back to the courage of this early man of God, and rejoice in the heroism with which he dared to rise to prove his faith and to rid his people of the detested Midianites who fully intended to destroy them.

Jephthah

Father: *Gilead*

Mother: *A harlot*

Place: *Gilead or Perea to the east of Jordan River*

Scripture: *Judges 11:1—12:7*

Jephthah, the son of Gilead by a strange woman who bore him and then turned him over to his father to rear, was resented by his legitimate half brother who drove him out. Thereupon he went to live in the land of Tob. There he seems to have applied himself to those skills which would be of the greatest value for a military life. Very likely he learned how to ride, how to throw the spear and the javelin, how to fight.

Then came the day for which any man who has ever been wronged longs. The elders of Gilead came, asking that he come to help them fight the Ammonites, who were annoying them. Jephthah weighed their proposition very carefully. He wanted to know if he would be ostracized when the battle was over, or if he would be given the rule over them and be granted social acceptance. He was assured that he would be accorded these benefits, and an agreement was reached.

Jephthah's technique seems to have been one of trying to avoid war if at all possible. In careful communications with the king of the Ammonites he sought to set forth the original situation that had prevailed at the time that the children of Israel had come up from the land of Egypt. He pointed out

68

that the Israelites were eager to pass through the land without trouble, whereas the man who was then the king of the Ammonites would not have it so, with the result that there had been war. Furthermore, in his communiqués, Jephthah made it plain that if war must come, he would face it, for he had no intention of retracting his position since he believed that God was with him, that he would make possible a victory for Israel.

Jephthah made a promise to the LORD, "If thou wilt give the Ammonites into mine hand, then whoever comes forth from the doors of my house to meet me, when I return victorious from the Ammonites, shall be the LORD's, and I will offer him up for a burnt offering."

When he returned to his home the first one he saw was his only daughter. Jephthah had made an agreement with God and he would stick with it even if it hurt him unspeakably to do so. He had been allowed to win his battle, the victory had been overwhelming. Why it was that his daughter had to be the one who came out first from the city he could not quite understand, but rather than change his vow, or ask the LORD to forgive his foolish rashness, Jephthah made plans to have his only child sacrificed.

When she learned that her father had made this vow with the LORD, she immediately acquiesced. As a matter of fact, there was nothing else for her to do. The thing which her father had determined to do with her was entirely in his hands to decide, for in those days an individual was the property of his father or mother and any disposition whatsoever could be made of the man or woman according to the wish of the parent.

She had a strange request to make, however. Since she had never been given to a man and had never been able to fulfill the privilege of motherhood, she asked for a time of mourning apart with a group of her maiden companions. She was allowed to go to the mountains for two months and at the end of that time she returned and was offered as a burnt sacrifice.

In the time of early Israel it was the custom of the people to offer human sacrifice as a demonstration of their love for their various gods, a custom derived from the pagan worship of the Canaanites. Actually the decision made by Abraham not to offer Isaac upon the mountain had seemed to the people a mark of weakness, and as a token of his lack of faith in his god. Jephthah's sacrifice of his daughter was contrary to the prophetic tradition started by Abraham.

There is an interesting story of the use of linguistics connected with Jephthah. During one of his military engagements with the Ephraimites a test was devised to separate the friends from the enemies.

The Ephraimites were asked to speak the word "Shibboleth." They could not pronounce the "h" and so they said "Sibboleth" in reply. This speech defect revealed them as enemies and Jephthah slew forty-two thousand of them as a result.

Although he was a man of war, there is every reason to believe that Jephthah died a natural death. His contributions to the amalgamation of his people into a nation may have been more far-reaching than might appear on the surface. When people fight together, they often come to trust one another, and to work together after the conflict. It was so with the Israelites, and during the course of the next few decades they became a nation.

Samson

Father: *Manoah*

Mother: *Her identity is given only as "The wife of Manoah"*

Place: *In northern Palestine near Dan*

Scripture: *Judges 13:2—16:31*

The story of Samson's birth becomes a story within itself. The wife of Manoah was barren, and the angel of the LORD appeared to her and told her that she should bear a son. He was to be reared as a Nazirite, and neither razor nor shears were to touch his hair.

The angel of the LORD told Manoah's wife that all these wonderful things were to be hers, but he refused to eat with her and her family. As they prepared a kid and a cereal offering for the LORD, the heavenly messenger disappeared in the flame.

The child was born, and was given the name of Samson. The text says, "The LORD blessed him. And the Spirit of the LORD began to stir him in Mahaneh-dan, between Zorah and Eshtaol." (Judges 13:24b-25a.) He seems very early to have manifested the extraordinary powers and blessings which truly were his in the years ahead.

Women were his weakness. It was on the way to Timnah that he saw one of the Philistine women and he returned to his father and asked him to buy the woman for him, or to make whatever marriage arrangements were necessary. We are told specifically that all this was of the LORD "for he was seeking an occasion against the Philistines. At that time the Philistines had dominion over Israel." (Judges 14:4.)

The father and mother went to Timnah with him to make these arrangements. En route there was a young lion that roared, and the little party heard it. Samson killed it, but said nothing to his parents about it.

Apparently this was a preliminary arrangement about the contract for the marriage, and it was some time later that the family went down again to claim the bride. On his way Samson saw that the carcass of the lion was there, and that a swarm of bees had made a honeycomb of it. He ate of the honey and gave some to his parents but did not mention where he got it.

It often happens that a person who is resourceful in one field, will try to demonstrate his prowess in another, only to fail miserably. This is what happened in the case of the big strong man. He thought that he would demonstrate what a mental tower he was. At the wedding feast he made a wager. He said that he would tell them a riddle. If they were able collectively to answer the question, he would give a suit of clothes to every one of the thirty men; but if they were unable to answer, each of them would have to give him a suit. They accepted the wager, but were unable to think of the answer to his puzzle, which was:

"Out of the eater came something to eat.
Out of the strong came something sweet."

The guests proceeded then to hound the bride. They told her they would burn her and her father's house if she did not get the answer from Samson. So she wheedled and she whined and she deviled the poor man until on the last day he gave her the answer. Immediately she told the wedding guests, who in turn told Samson that nothing was sweeter than honey, nothing stronger than a lion. In fury Samson went out and killed thirty men of Ashkelon and robbed them of their clothes to pay his wager.

When Samson came again to see his wife, he found that her father had turned her over to another man. He was furious once more, and this time used the most cunning device for bringing havoc among the Philistines. He caught three hundred foxes, tied them together by their tails, and put a firebrand to each. Then he turned them loose and, of course, the result was that they fired the fields of the Philistines, and brought havoc to their crops. The Philistines were quite unhappy about this business, and they came and burned Samson's wife and his father-in-law.

When Samson heard of this, he was even more enraged, and "he smote them hip and thigh with a great slaughter." He wrought great confusion and bloodshed. Immediately the Philistines gathered, and when the men of Judah saw them, they asked why the Philistines were there. The answer was that they had come for Samson, and they intended to get him.

"Swear to me that you will not fall upon me yourselves," Samson made the Judahites promise; and when they did promise, he permitted them to tie his hands with new cords, and they brought him up from the rock of Etam. There they must have held some sort of court, for the Philistines shouted against Samson, and the text says, "The Spirit of the LORD came mightily upon him, and the ropes which were on his arms became as flax that has caught fire, and his bonds melted off his hands." Then Samson took the jawbone of an ass which he found nearby, and with it slew a thousand men. After this he was extremely thirsty, and God split open a hollow place and water gushed forth. Samson drank and was refreshed. (Judges 15: 18-19.)

Next he went to Gaza where he took up with a harlot. During the night, because no man dared to come upon him alone, the men of the city shut the city gates on him intending to waylay him in the morning. Yet when Samson awoke and found that the city gates were locked, he simply lifted them up posts and all, and took them to the foot of Hebron, a distance of approximately thirty miles.

It was with Delilah, however, a woman in the valley of Sorek, that he met his Waterloo. She, too, seems to have been an adventuress for there is no statement to the effect that she was his wife. The infatuation apparently was one-sided. Samson was like one under a spell. Delilah, on the other hand, had a contract with the leaders of the Philistines that each of them would pay her eleven hundred pieces of silver if she would discover a weakness in him by which they could overpower him. We have a Mata Hari at work upon this strong but foolish man.

The revelation of the actual source of his strength was not made at once, and it seems that after three tries Samson should have caught on to the fact that Delilah was determined to ruin him. When Delilah first tried to find the source of his strength, Samson told her that he would become weak if he were bound with seven fresh bowstrings which had not been dried. But when she bound him with the fresh bowstrings, he snapped them with one movement. Then he told her that his strength would leave if he were bound with new ropes but again he broke the ropes "like a thread." Next he told her that weaving the seven locks of his hair into a web and fastening it with a pin would do the trick but when he awoke, he pulled away the pin and web. Delilah then told him that he could not love her if he would not tell her truly wherein his strength lay. Then he admitted that he had been a Nazirite from birth and had never had his hair shaved, saying that if he were shaved, his strength would leave him. This admission proved his undoing, for when Samson was asleep, Delilah summoned the Philistines who paid her the money that they had promised her. They furnished a barber who cut Samson's locks. His strength left him.

The Philistines seized Samson, put out his eyes, and bound him with fetters of bronze and put him in the prison house to grind.

Finally as time passed his hair grew again and the spirit of the LORD returned to him. At a great religious celebration at Gaza, when the Philistines were to have a feast to Dagon, they summoned Samson to entertain them. His stunt was to be one in which he would demonstrate his tremendous strength. They put him at the focal point in the building between the two supporting pillars. Then Samson prayed, "O Lord God, remember me, I pray thee, and strengthen me, I pray thee, only this once, O God." (Judges 16:28.) Samson then bowed himself and caused the house to fall upon the 3,000 people assembled there.

Thus Samson met his death along with more of the Philistines than he had slain during the course of his whole life.

Ruth

Father: *Not known*

Mother: *Not known*

Place: *Judea and Trans-Jordan in what is known as the land of Moab*

Scripture: *The Book of Ruth*

While the little Book of Ruth is thought to deal primarily with the character of Ruth, actually it deals almost as much with the experiences of a woman named Naomi, who was born a generation earlier.

Migration in those days was easy. The people went where they thought they could live, and this was largely determined by good crops and by droughts. The unfavorable situation in Judah prompted Naomi and her husband to go eastward into Moab where they lived a while. There Elimelech, the husband, died. Meanwhile their two sons, Mahlon and Chilion, had come to man's estate, and had married Moabitish women. Mahlon married Ruth, Chilion married Orpah.

After a few years the two young men died, and the three widows were left to face the world. Naomi decided that she would return to Judah. The two daughters-in-law started back with her. When she bade them farewell, she explained that it was no longer possible for her to rear up sons to be their husbands. Even if it were possible, she was sure that they would not want to wait as long a time as that would take. According to the custom then in vogue when a man died, his brother was supposed to take his wife and to rear up children to his memory.

At Naomi's suggestion Orpah returned to the land of Moab where it is to be supposed that she married and lived the remainder of her life among her people. Ruth, however, clung to her mother-in-law with the statement which has attracted the imagination of people of every generation from then till now, "Entreat me not to leave you or to return from following you; for where you go I will go, and where you lodge I will lodge; your people shall be my people, and your God my God; where you die I will die, and there will I be buried. May the LORD do so to me and more also if even death parts me from you." (Ruth 1:16-17.)

Thus the two widows entered the land of Judah where Naomi proceeded to arrange for a second marriage of her daughter-in-law. Ruth had to work, and inasmuch as it was the time of harvest when they arrived, she went to the field of one Boaz, a man of some means who was supervising the work in his fields. She made such a good impression upon him that he invited her to continue to glean there in his own plot, and at mealtime asked her to share in the meal afforded to the workers. She thanked him and stayed. During the afternoon Boaz told some of the reapers to let fall special sheaves in her way so that she might have them.

Evidently there was an age difference between Boaz and Ruth. He seems to have been fully old enough to be her father, for the text speaks of the "younger men," in several instances. This would hint at the fact that Ruth would naturally have turned to younger men, or men of her own age, whereas her attitude toward Boaz indicates that he must have been much older than she.

Naomi was pleased with the fact that Boaz noticed Ruth and and that he liked her. But it was time to make some decision in the matter of their relationships. That night Naomi directed

Ruth to go to the field where Boaz was to sleep, and to observe where he put his pallet. When Boaz fell asleep, she was to uncover his feet as a gesture of willingness to marry. She did these things. When Boaz awakened and saw his feet exposed, he supposed that there was danger afoot. He found with relief that it was the Moabite woman who had slept beside him. He was pleased that she was there, and he told her to bide the night, saying that on the morrow he would complete the legal arrangements for securing her for his wife.

In those days there was the custom of inheriting the responsibilities of household and family as well as the property. In this case Boaz recognized that the connections with Naomi were legal, and that the next of kin would have prior rights in the matter of "selling" or "buying" the woman in marriage. Thus it was that he went into the city, and seated himself near the gate, and when the people came by he asked that they step aside and be seated. When the next of kin came by, Boaz proposed that this man should buy Elimelech's land, and that either he should pay the necessary amount for the widow's dower, or that he should let Boaz buy it. The next of kin was favorable to the idea of making up the dower himself, but lacked the ready cash to clinch the deal. He made profound apologies, and asked Boaz if he would like to redeem his inheritance. Boaz bought the rights from this man and claimed Ruth as his own wife. The deal was signed, sealed, and delivered by the unique method of the next of kin taking off his shoe and giving it to Boaz. If ever any question should arise as to the transaction, there would be witnesses who would recall that they had seen the deal. Then, too, Boaz had the extra proof in the possession of the man's shoe, and if the shoe fit, that would be proof positive that the transaction had been made earlier.

Then Boaz made his proclamation to the witnesses: "You are witnesses this day that I have bought from the hand of Naomi all that belonged to Elimelech and all that belonged to

Chilion and to Mahlon. Also Ruth the Moabitess, the widow of Mahlon, I have bought to be my wife, to perpetuate the name of the dead in his inheritance, that the name of the dead may not be cut off from among his brethren and from the gate of his native place; you are witnesses this day." (Ruth 4:9-10.)

This pleased the people, and they blessed the marriage, and Boaz took Ruth to be his wife, and she bore him a child named Obed, who was the grandfather of David.

Samuel

Father: *Elkanah*

Mother: *Hannah*

Place: *Palestine*

Scripture: *1 Samuel 1:20—25:1*

Samuel was born in a time when Eli was the priest in Israel. Eli was a man of tremendous power, a kindly and a discerning soul, whose sons were thoroughly immoral, and a constant embarrassment to their father.

Elkanah, Samuel's father, who was a faithful worshiper of God, came annually to the temple to present his family before the LORD. He had two wives, of whom Hannah seems to have been the favorite, but she was barren. While at the temple one day, she vowed that if only she could have a son, she would forthwith dedicate him to the service of the LORD. Eli rebuked her for being drunk. She insisted that she was not drunk, but that she had been at prayer. Even as she prayed, she was assured that the child would be given and soon she brought forth her first-born son, to whom she gave the name "Samuel," which means "asked of God."

In the course of a while this child was brought to the temple to be reared in the total life of the religious work.

It is interesting that the text mentions the way in which the priest was paid in those days. "The custom of the priests with the people was that when any man offered sacrifice, the priest's servant would come, while the meat was boiling, with a three-pronged fork in his hand, and he would thrust it into the pan, or kettle, or cauldron, or pot; all that the fork brought up the priest would take for himself." (1 Samuel 2:13-14.) It was because of this very arrangement of the priest's portion, that the sons of Eli got into trouble because they wrangled with the worshipers, asking for fresh uncooked meats, and calling for the choice parts of the meat.

Samuel, so innocent in his own right and so very devoted to the sacredness of his holy office, was aware that Eli was growing blind. One night, as the lad slept, he heard the voice of the LORD calling, but he thought that it was the voice of Eli, and went to the latter's bedside, only to be told twice to go back to bed and to sleep. Finally it dawned upon Eli what was happening, and he told the lad to answer the voice and to say, "Speak, LORD, for thy servant hears." The LORD called to Samuel yet the third time and told him that Eli's sons would not rise to be judges of Israel after him because they had failed in their ministrations at the temple. The next morning when Eli inquired as to what the LORD had revealed, Samuel told him, and the old man was reconciled. He felt no resentment that his sons were not to ascend to the holy office, and no jealousy that this particular youth was to become the great prophet of Israel.

Samuel became the judge who followed Eli, for that good man, upon learning of the outcome of the battle with the Philistines, in which both his sons, Hophni and Phinehas, were killed, reared back in his seat upon the city's wall, lost his balance, and fell several feet to the ground. There it was discovered that he . had broken his neck and died.

The ark of the covenant of the LORD was thought to have all manner of amazing properties. It was first of all a blessing to Israel, and the people of Israel expected it to deliver them from their enemies. Second, when it was captured, it was supposed to serve as a curse to the enemy—for example, all of the people of Gath suffered from tumors. (1 Samuel 5:9.) The

81

Philistines, therefore, determined to be rid of the religious piece, and they prepared to return it, and did so with five golden tumors and five golden mice—their way of saying that one was for Ashdod, one for Gaza, one for Ashkelon, one for Gath, and one for Ekron. The ark and the box of golden figures were put on a cart to which were yoked two milch cows without their calves. The cows lowed all the way across the territorial line, as they came to the field of Joseph of Bethshemesh. The men of that place rounded up and slaughtered the cows and offered them as a sacrifice to God. Thus in their thinking was restitution made that the precious ark was returned with guilt offerings from the Philistines.

When Samuel became old, the elders of Israel asked him to appoint a king to govern them. Monarchy was having its way among the people, and the people of Israel were determined in their thinking that for reasons of military security, and for the establishment of a court similar to those of the other kingdoms around and about, they must have a king.

Samuel prayed to the LORD who said, "Hearken to their voice, and make them a king."

Samuel's sons, Joel and Abijah, were unscrupulous men not suited to rule. They took bribes and set themselves up as venders of decisions, rather than as judges of equity and right.

It was through Samuel's influence that Saul became the king selected, and still later, it was again the influence of Samuel that decided the issue against Saul, and that turned the people toward the consideration of David as the successor to the throne.

Samuel and Saul definitely disagreed over several things. First there was the clash over the matter of the holy office. Once when Saul had called the people together and Samuel was late in getting to the feast to offer the blessing for it, Saul offered the thanks himself. Samuel resented this encroachment upon his priestly function. (1 Samuel 13:9 ff.) Then there was the matter of obedience to the stipulation of Samuel that the Amalekites were to be destroyed—" 'both man and woman, infant and suckling, ox and sheep, camel and ass,'" but Saul kept the sheep, oxen, fatlings, and lambs, which infuriated Samuel. He said,

> "Behold, to obey is better than sacrifice,
>   and to hearken better than the fat of rams."

Samuel himself had Agag brought before him and he hewed Agag in pieces before the LORD in Gilgal. (1 Samuel 15:33a.)

As a result of these clashes between Samuel and Saul, the old priest was influenced to anoint David as the successor to the throne. (At the time when Samuel asked the people to witness against him if at any time he had taken an ox, an ass, or defrauded or oppressed any or had received bribes, the people declared that at no time had he defrauded or oppressed, or had he taken aught of any man. See 1 Samuel 12:3-4.)

Thus Samuel lived his life and passed from the scene. His home was at Ramah where he lies buried.

Saul

Father: *Kish*

Mother: *Not known*

Place: *Palestine*

Scripture: *1 Samuel 9:1—31:7*

Saul is introduced in the Scriptures as a young man who was dispatched to find three asses that had strayed. He trailed them through the land of Shaalim and through the land of Zuph and found no trace of them. Then he decided to search for Samuel, a man of God who was supposed to be able to do all manner of amazing things, such as finding lost articles, lost persons, and so forth, and to wield tremendous influence.

When the question arose as to being able to pay the man of God, it was found that Saul did not have a red cent. One of the servants who went along with Saul had a coin, a fourth part of a shekel of silver. This Saul promptly borrowed, and they set out to find the prophet (or the seer as he was sometimes called in those days) to tell where the asses might be.

Against the background of this experience was the growing sentiment in Israel that the land should be changed from a theocracy or a land ruled by priests to a monarchy which would provide many phases of protection, much prestige, and definite national unity. Samuel had been thinking in terms of a king for the people, and the LORD told Samuel that he would meet such a man to make the future king. Thus Saul was seeking Samuel, and Samuel was seeking Saul. Samuel reported immediately that the three asses had been found, and entertained the lad, giving him the seat of honor at the feast which was in progress upon the mountaintop. When they came down, Samuel talked with Saul and anointed him with oil.

The effect of the anointing with oil seems to have loosed Saul's tongue, for he began to speak with tremendous fervor, and the people were so amazed at the things that he said, that they exclaimed, "Is Saul also among the prophets?" (1 Samuel 10:12.) This same experience seems to have come years later when Saul prophesied. (Compare 1 Samuel, chapters 18—24.)

When Saul returned to his father's house, his uncle questioned him as to why he had been away so long. Saul told about the finding of the stray asses but he was silent about the conversation with Samuel, and about his being anointed as the future king of Israel.

In 1 Samuel, chapter 10, there is the reproof of the people at the hand of Samuel, because of the people's desire for a king to rule over Israel; and yet with reproof, it was Samuel's immediate decision to tell the people just who was to be that king. This was accomplished by three means. First the tribes passed, and the tribe of Benjamin was chosen; then the families of that tribe passed and the family of Matri was chosen; and finally Saul was chosen. Saul had hidden himself among the household stuff, and when he was brought forth, he was head and shoulders taller than the rest of the men of Isarel. At his appearance the people raised a mighty shout and cried, "Long live the king!"

The very fact that Saul had been selected by Samuel did not quite *establish* Saul as the new king. Sometimes it seems that such selections have to be bathed in blood. In this instance it happened that there was a certain Nahash who was the captain of the Ammonites. He came with a sizable contingent of military men and the Hebrews, on seeing his strength, begged for a treaty to work for Nahash as slaves. Nahash told that each of them must submit to having one eye thrust out. Thus the children of Israel would be a marked people, a one-eyed group of men and women. They asked for seven days of grace before they would submit, and Nahash granted them this period in which to consider his terms.

Immediately some of the men of Jabesh-gilead came to Saul, and told him of the threat and of their hopeless condition. At the moment Saul was plowing a field. He slew his oxen on the spot, sent the parts to the groups of Israelites round about, and said, "Whoever does not come out after Saul and Samuel, so shall it be done to his oxen!" The men rallied instantly. Then Saul divided the 330,000 who answered the call into three groups, and so arranged his attack and so successfully prosecuted the engagement that the few enemies who survived were scattered. This victory established Saul as the undisputed leader of the nation.

The first instance of trouble between the aged judge and the young king seems to have come at the time of one of the religious festivals. Seven days the people waited for Samuel to come, and when he did not appear, Saul himself proceeded with the feast. When Samuel did arrive, he was incensed, and assured Saul that the LORD would punish him sorely. It was no idle threat, for Samuel proceeded to anoint David as the future king of Israel.

The next clash between Samuel and Saul resulted from the warfare with Agag, the Amalekite. In this engagement Samuel told Saul that he must obliterate every man, woman, child, and every living thing. Agag, however, seemed to Saul to be a good piece of booty, and the people looked like reasonably profitable slaves, so Saul spared some of their lives. When Samuel found out about this, he was furious and declared that Saul would rue the day of his refusal to obey the word of God. Then when Saul entreated Samuel to recall the statement, and sought to make right the matter in the sight of God, Saul grabbed Samuel and tore the skirt of his robe. Samuel declared that the kingdom of Israel was torn from him that very day.

Samuel was indeed a man of tremendously strong will, and he insisted that Agag be brought before him, and there, before the people and standing where Saul could see, he hewed Agag to pieces.

Samuel did not see Saul again during his lifetime. After Samuel had died and when Saul wanted help and guidance as to how to deal with David, he sought out the woman of Endor and had her recall the spirit of Samuel. Saul hoped for help but Samuel remained at odds with him, and declared that God would wrest the kingdom from his hands and would give it to the more youthful and more brilliant David.

Saul suffered a torment which seems to have been the source of a great deal of trouble. When the vicious seizures came upon him, he could be quieted by music. Thus was brought into the circle of Saul's life the lad who in manhood would torment him and would eventually take his kingdom. David was the sweet singer and soothed the heart of Saul with his music. (1 Samuel 16:14-23.)

Saul upon meeting Goliath was made to feel very helpless before the giant. (Read chapter 17.) All the methods of dueling that Saul knew and all the methods of combat upon which he relied were useless against this super man. David offered to kill the giant. Saul handed his own uniform and his own battle garb to David but David was not used to these things, and so David went to meet the giant just as he had been garbed all along. When David killed the giant, there followed such a victory as heartened Israel, and filled the hearts of the people with great joy. They sang, but the words of their song brought no joy to Saul's ears for they sang:

"Saul has slain his thousands,
And David his tens of thousands."

When David returned to the palace, Saul in a moment of rage thrust a javelin at him, and would have killed him had not David jumped aside.

Saul sought to humiliate David. He promised him Merab, one of Saul's daughters, and then gave her to another man. However, Michal, one of the younger daughters of Saul, loved David, and she became David's wife. Then when Jonathan and Michal befriended David and actually saved his life, Saul became so enraged that he cast his spear twice at Jonathan and would have nailed him to the wall with it if he could.

The guerrilla warfare that characterized the whole reign of Saul was of a dangerous order, and the rivalry of David and Saul brought weakness and bloodshed. Together they could have united Israel, but their constant fighting of each other weakened Israel greatly. Saul tried by every means he knew to kill David. David tried to weaken Saul, but avoided killing him because, as he said, Saul was the LORD's anointed. This "anointed" business was a part of his own experience, and he cast a veritable aura around it. Thus it was a means of protection for himself.

Just before Saul's death, he and David seem to have been reconciled, but the benefits of this reconciliation meant little. They were shortly at odds with one another, and this time Abishai who was the confederate of David had the opportunity to kill the old king, but David insisted that he must be spared because he was the LORD's anointed. So Saul's spear and jar of water were stolen that Saul might realize that David again could have taken his life.

Many military men down through the centuries have taken their own lives rather than throw themselves upon the mercy of their enemies. In one of the engagements with the Philistines, Saul saw three of his sons butchered—Jonathan, Abinadab, and Malchishua. He knew that he himself did not have a chance, so he ordered his armor-bearer to kill him. This he refused to do, so Saul took his own sword and fell upon it. The armor-bearer, with no hopes of mercy, killed himself.

Jonathan

Father: *Saul*

Mother: *Not known*

Place: *Palestine*

Scripture: *1 Samuel 13:2—2 Samuel 1:17*

Jonathan was by rights the first of the princes of Israel, and should to all intents and purposes have succeeded his father as the king.

He was a lad of approximately the same age as David, and he might have been exceedingly jealous of the young competitor for public favor. Such was not his nature, however, for we find that Jonathan loved David and befriended him.

Jonathan was a capable leader of men in battle as is exemplified by the fact that in Gibeah of Benjamin, he led the armies with distinction to total victory.

Later during this same campaign when the Philistines had gathered in such numbers that the people of Israel were alarmed and many of them fled to Gad, Jonathan stayed with his father, and seizing a moment when the thing could be done, he and his armor-bearer went around to the rear of the lines of the Philistines and so used the protection of the terrain that they were able to slay twenty of the Philistines before a general alarm was given. This was a brave move, and Jonathan managed to escape with his armor-bearer. When he got back to camp, he ate some honey. This was a violation of his father's order for that day that no man eat for twenty-four hours, as a fast.

Saul condemned Jonathan and in all probability the king would have had him killed on the spot if it had not been that the men were so enthusiastic about what a heroic thing he had done that they raised a solid wall of protest before Saul, and made him back down from his decision. (Read 1 Samuel, chapter 14.)

There is every reason to believe that Jonathan was his father's right-hand man during the full course of his reign. At the time when the army of Saul was defeated by the Philistines, Jonathan fell in battle. (1 Samuel 31:2.) He and his father were buried in the same service, and they received honors at the hand of David at the same time. (2 Samuel 1:17.)

The mention of David and Jonathan comes readily to the tongue for the two young men were exceedingly fond of one another. The text says, "the soul of Jonathan was knit with the soul of David, and Jonathan loved him as his own soul." (1 Samuel 18:1.)

Jonathan seemed to show the greater measure of devotion. It was Jonathan who gave the gifts, Jonathan who entrusted David with his own sword, and with his own bow, and his own girdle.

When Saul commissioned Jonathan to search out David as a man utterly dangerous to the security of the throne, Jonathan found David, but told him to be on his guard for his father was determined to seek his life to kill him. (1 Samuel 19:2.) This was a terrific breach of military confidence, and can be accounted for only on the grounds of the man's overwhelming devotion to David.

Then Jonathan persuaded his father to become reconciled with this unruly young man, and David came back into the court as the singer and the soothing agent for Saul's troubled spirit. Yet while Saul sat listening to David sing, he toyed all the while with his spear, and suddenly hurled it with all his strength at David who would have been pinned to the wall if he had not been agile enough to get away.

That night Michal, who was Saul's daughter and David's wife, helped him gain distance by putting a dummy into bed, and claiming that the stuffed image was David, and that he was sick.

At a rendezvous David met Jonathan, and Jonathan promised to give full help to David. There is not one record of any failure on the part of this son of Saul to carry out the fullest spirit of his agreements. Following this meeting a second meeting was planned to show David whether or not to flee from Saul permanently. Jonathan planned to shoot three arrows to the side of the rock where David was hiding and then to send a boy to pick them up. If he said to the lad, "Look, the arrows are on this side of you, take them," it would be safe for David to stay. But if his comment was "Look, the arrows are beyond you," David would have to flee. The report was unfavorable and the two friends bade each other a sorrowful farewell.

Jonathan met him later at a time when it would have been greatly to the advantage of the government for Jonathan to have remained loyal to the throne, and there in the wood, Jonathan said to David, "Fear not; for the hand of Saul my father shall not find you; and you shall be king over Israel, and I shall be next to you; Saul my father also knows this." (1 Samuel 23:17.)

When Jonathan died, he left a five-year-old son, a cripple, by the name of Mephibosheth. (2 Samuel 4:4.) This child was sought out by David, and was allowed to eat at David's table in remembrance of his father. This represented a perfectly harmless relationship, for there was no possibility of a man with his physical handicap ever leading troops, and that was an essential in David's time.

David

Father: *Jesse*

Mother: *Not known*

Place: *Palestine*

Scripture: *Ruth 4:22; 1 Samuel 16:8—1 Kings 2*

There is something dashing and fascinating about David. He managed to combine the lovable qualities of a noble spirit with the unpredictable doings of a desperado. His charm as a singer of sacred hymns was matched with his ability as a seducer of beautiful women. His bravado was exceeded only by his ability to repent. No man ever fascinated the Jews more completely, and no leader among them was ever more loved.

David, the son of Jesse, was a shepherd lad—talented, strong, alert, and of a splendid mind. Upon the throne sat a man whose "spells" were a problem to the doctors. Soothing music upon the harp, with gentle singing, seemed to soothe the king, and this lad was brought to play before Saul as one of the court entertainers. He made a good impression and was well received.

Saul, however, had troubles other than illness. The Philistines who inhabited the country along with the Israelites banded themselves together, and presented a champion. The Philistines had Goliath who was more than a match for any man of Israel, and had Saul gone out to do battle with him according to the accepted methods of sportsmanship and warfare, he would have been killed in a moment.

David, a lad, saw, however, that with his slingshot he could kill the giant, and he offered to do battle. Had David said that he was going to fight with the sling, he would have been disqualified because that would not have been ethical technique of combat. This fact he kept to himself. He went into the no-man's land between the two armies, and there he watched as Goliath cursed and threw away his shield and sword, and took out after him to catch him and to spank him thoroughly. David took this opportunity to place his shot deep into the forehead of the defenseless man. (1 Samuel 17:49.)

The excitement was so great that the ethics were forgotten, and the men seized the opportunity, and dashed in to destroy the Philistines.

Saul was pleased at first. He honored David, and he sought to be gracious. But the praise David received got the better of Saul and his jealous nature reacted violently. Deliberately he tried to pin David to the wall with his javelin.

From being the favored one in the court, David became the one whose life was in the gravest danger. It was in this circumstance that the true character of the man Jonathan came to the front. While Jonathan was in line for the throne and should have succeeded his father as king, according to the rule of inheritance, he actually became the greatest of all the enthusiasts over the young David. Their friendship stands as a model to this day. Instead of being jealous of the evident popularity of this adventurer, Jonathan protected him against the determinations of his father.

What actually happened was that David gathered to himself a group of adventurers, and they put themselves against Saul, the king. They made a sort of guerrilla warfare throughout the land, and succeeded in weakening the power of Saul to the place where eventually Saul was destroyed. This did not happen all at once, but as the result of David's incessant attacks, and of Saul's having to fight the Philistines. The drain upon Saul's manpower and upon his resources was too heavy, and David effected a successful revolt, for he took the throne.

David experienced many hair-breadth escapes during the course of this. Once when David was hungry, he and his men ate the holy bread in the temple; another time David was at the end of his resources and he escaped to the camp of the people of Gath. There he feigned madness, let the saliva run down his beard, and acted as if he were totally and completely insane. This saved his life. Again he escaped to live in a cave, the cave of Adullam, but in this instance he managed to gather to himself all the malcontents. All those who resented the authority of Saul came to David, and he built quite a following for himself. Saul learned of his whereabouts and came to attack him but David escaped. In the course of the efforts to get him, David was so near that twice he could have taken Saul's life. In one instance he cut off Saul's skirt and in the other David took Saul's spear and the cruse of water from Saul's tent. In both instances David insisted that Saul's life be spared because Saul was one of the LORD's anointed and to touch a hair of the head of one of the LORD's anointed was unthinkable. Actually this became a means of self-protection to David, because he was himself one of the anointed.

The culmination of these activities came when Saul and Jonathan were killed in an engagement with the Philistines.

Immediately David became the king of Judah and in the course of some eighteen months he became the king of Israel.

One of the things that David did to make possible his undisputed authority in the kingdom was to wipe out the heirs of Saul. There were two sons of Saul by a concubine whose name was Rizpah, and five grandsons of Saul by Merab. David turned them over to the Gibionites who hanged them. Rizpah came and stayed nearly ninety days watching those bodies lest the birds by day or beasts by night should touch them.

Undoubtedly many of these relationships seem strange to us now. Here follow the women who had a place in David's life:

Merab: This was one of Saul's daughters. She was promised to David, but when the time came for her to be

given to him she was given to Adriel the Mehola-
thite as an insult to David.

Michal: This was another of Saul's daughters. This girl
loved David deeply, and saved his life upon one
occasion by substituting a dummy in the bed, and
saying that David was sick. During some of the
warfare between her father and her husband she
stayed with her father and was given in marriage
to this same Adriel who was her sister's husband
and to whom she bore five sons. At another time
she seems to have been given to Palti. When
David danced before the ark of the covenant, she
showed her displeasure, and David ostracized her
from that time.

Abigail: David came to know this woman through a dispute
between his soldiers and Abigail's husband whose
name was Nabal. She came to David's tent and
apologized for the misunderstanding and for the
fact that Nabal had opposed David's soldiers.
David accepted the food she brought and she left
in peace. That very day, however, Nabal was
taken sick, and ten days later he died. Immediately David and Abigail became husband and wife.

Ahinoam: There is little way of knowing how many wives
David had. The text merely says that "David took
Ahinoam of Jezreel."

Bathsheba: This beautiful woman was the wife of one of the
members of David's army. While her husband was
away, David saw her bathing and had her brought
to the palace, for David had a house built as his
palace. There was no promise of marriage in this
arrangement. When Uriah, Bathsheba's husband,
came into town with the troops, David sent for
him and kept him at the palace until he returned
to the battle. David sent word to his commanding

95

general to have Uriah put into the thick of the next fight and to see to it that he was killed. This was done and Bathsheba became David's wife. Nathan, the old prophet, denounced David to his face for this sin, and told him that his first child would die. David fasted and prayed during the child's illness but the LORD did not hear him. Solomon was the second child by this woman, and through her influence with the self-same Nathan, Solomon was later crowned successor to David's throne.

There were undoubtedly elements of greatness in the life of David. He had a job of pioneering to accomplish, and he worked with every means at his command. He ruled for forty years. His songs will live forever as classics. There was a religious fervor about this man, a remarkable humanness which appealed greatly to his people.

It was not easy to be a ruler in his day. His own son Absalom tried to steal the throne and did succeed in driving David into hiding, but Absalom was not able to hold the power, and was not able to win the confidence of the people, and for that reason his revolt came to nothing, and he, himself, was caught by his own hair in a tree and there hung until Joab came and killed him. (2 Samuel 18:14.)

Such experiences are not easy, and yet as David came through each trial, he managed to find for himself a place of even greater security in the hearts of his people.

Nathan

Father: *Not known*

Mother: *Not known*

Place: *Palestine*

Scripture: *2 Samuel, chapter 7; 12:1-25; 1 Kings 1:34; 1 Chronicles 29:29; 2 Chronicles 9:29*

Israel was ever respectful of her prophets. These men were strange in their manner and in their dress. Theirs was not a settled ministry. They did not fill pulpits. They never knew from day to day where their next meal would come from. It was a thankless job to be a prophet in Israel. Generally they represented the reforming element. They were the men who were always and forever criticizing whatever was done.

They dressed shabbily, they ate anything and everything. They were extraordinary men, and they proclaimed their message with an emphasis that cannot be forgotten because it was decidedly effective.

Nathan was one of the earlier among these men.

In the early days of the kingdom, Nathan made himself known as a prophet in Israel. He wandered about preaching as he pleased, saying whatsoever he chose, and managing to hold respect wherever he went.

David had become the king and had built himself a house of cedar. This represented quite a step forward, inasmuch as Israel had always dwelt in tents. He began to think about the tabernacle, which was a tent. Surely if he had a better house

97

for himself than he had for his God, there was something wrong. Consequently David broached the subject to the prophet, Nathan, the next time he saw him, and said, "See now, I dwell in an house of cedar, but the ark of God dwells in a tent." (2 Samuel 7:1-3.)

The prophet replied that this sounded reasonable, and that he would do whatever seemed right in his own sight.

That night, however, Nathan received word from the LORD that David was not to be allowed to build the house for the LORD, for this was be one of the responsibilities for the son of David. Wrapped up in the same direction was the promise that David's line should be established in Israel and that the rule of the people should be in his family.

David regretted that he himself would not be privileged to build the LORD's house, but he was pleased that his descendants were to reign through the years. Thus, out of a very full heart David came before the LORD and made his prayer of thanksgiving. This is a classic of great beauty and begins: "Who am I, O LORD GOD, and what is my house, that thou hast brought me thus far?" (2 Samuel 7:18-29.)

To appreciate the significance of Nathan's appearance before David, one must bear in mind the fact that David was an absolute monarch. He had complete control in matters of life and death. There was no such thing as trial by jury; there was no such thing as a body of law which served as a bulwark of protection for the people. David could have given the word and Nathan would have been killed, or would have been starved to death, or would have been flayed alive.

The circumstance is well known. David had seen a very beautiful woman whose husband was in David's army. The husband was away with the troops, David saw this beautiful creature and had her come to the palace, and they became lovers.

David arranged with Joab to have Uriah, the husband, put right into the thick of the next engagement, and to have him killed.

This being done, David thought the business was very nicely handled, and that he was through with it all. What he overlooked was the fact that there were prophets in Israel. Nathan came into the town and came before David, the king.

Just how Nathan made his approach to the subject, is lost to history. Certainly he opened the subject of his appeal in masterly fashion, by telling the king how one of his subjects, who had many lambs and great wealth, had seized the lone pet of a very poor man and had taken this pet to offer as a meal for his guests. David was furious, and declared that the wealthy man would pay to the uttermost, that he would be made to restore fourfold. Then with a voice that trembled with emotion he demanded to know the man's name.

To have Nathan say, "You are the man" was a blow that David had not expected, and it shook him as he had never dreamed that he could be shaken. The damnableness of his sin came home to him. He was shocked. Yes, he had taken Bathsheba to the palace, and she was now one of the women of his household. She was already with child. Nathan declared that this child would die, and surely enough this came to pass. David prayed for a full week, he draped himself in sackcloth and ashes, and he fasted—but to no avail. The child did die. (2 Samuel 12:1-23.)

For all of his fiery nature, however, Nathan was a friendly and an influential person. When Bathsheba brought forth her next child, Nathan took particular notice of the little one. David and Bathsheba called their newborn son Solomon and the old prophet gave him the very special name of Jedidiah which means "beloved of the LORD." (2 Samuel 12:24-25.)

Nathan watched as this child grew. He observed the ambitions of the several sons of David as they sought for preferment.

When David was dying, Nathan stepped into the picture as the champion of Bathsheba's child, Solomon, and maneuvered this lad into the kingship.

Adonijah, who was also a son of David, was seeking to establish himself as the king while his father lay dying. While he gathered many of the leaders of Israel, Nathan teamed up with Zadok, the priest, and the two of them went before David as the sponsors of Solomon. Thus even while the great gathering of Adonijah's friends was taking place, Nathan engineered a coup, and by David's authority arranged to have Solomon anointed, and to have him ride through the town on the king's mule. (1 Kings, chapter 1.)

Solomon

Father: *David*

Mother: *Bathsheba*

Place: *Palestine*

Scripture: *2 Samuel 5:14—2 Chronicles 9:29; Songs of Solomon, Proverbs, and Ecclesiastes*

This second son of David and Bathsheba comes down to us through the long course of history as a genius par excellence. He is remembered not because of his wealth—although he was, after the fashion of oriental despots, a man of wealth and power—but because he was able to give a certain twist to his philosophy which delighted the hearts of the Jews. The things they had always thought, Solomon was able to say for them in terse sentences that even now stand among the choice maxims and proverbs of the world.

His possession of the throne came by right of inheritance. Solomon's father, David, had managed his own "election" to the throne by means of his strong right arm. Solomon, however, stepped into power by dint of a little astute political maneuvering on the part of his mother and Nathan, the prophet.

It was as the hour of David's end drew near and it was realized he was on his deathbed, that one of his sons named Adonijah decided that he would seize the throne. Adonijah conferred with Joab, and an ambitious priest named Abiathar, and both of these men declared that they would lend their support for his claims to the throne. (1 Kings 1:7.) It just so happened that Shimei and Rei, the incumbent priest named Zadok, Benaiah, a very influential priest, and Nathan, the firebrand prophet, did not approve.

Nathan instructed Bathsheba to go to plead for her son before David. Then he followed her there and broke the news of the hasty action on the part of Adonijah. David was aroused by all this, and commanded that Solomon ride through the city's street upon his own mule, and that Zadok, the priest, should anoint him king at Gihon. Then the people were to proclaim, "Long live King Solomon!"

This was done immediately and within hearing of the feast that Adonijah was having with his untried confederates.

When Adonijah realized what had happened, and when he realized that he had been bested by this younger half-brother, he rushed straight to the tabernacle where he grabbed hold of the horns upon the altar, and would not let go. (It was believed that to hold to the horns of the altar, was to keep one free from assault or murder.) When word reached Solomon that Adonijah was there, literally scared to death, he gave word that he should be told to go to his own house. This he did. But he should have known that his days were numbered, and that while Solomon might let him live for a little while, upon the first possible pretext Solomon would have him put to death in order to eliminate all claimants to the throne. This opportunity came when Adonijah asked Bathsheba to intercede for him that he might be given Abishag to wife. (This same Abishag had been the last wife of David.) Immediately Solomon seized upon this as sufficient excuse, and had him put to death.

There is indeed something pathetic about the mistrust and the crimes that followed in the course of each new ascendant to the throne. Actually the danger did not lie so much in power of the throne itself, as in the fact that it was impossible to get the incumbent out of office except by natural or unnatural death. Saul, David, and Solomon each spent forty years in this position.

102

Several stories are concerned with Solomon's wisdom. The first is that of a dream in which the LORD appeared to Solomon and asked him what he would like to have. Solomon answered, "O LORD my God, thou hast made thy servant king. . . . Give thy servant therefore an understanding mind to govern thy people, that I may discern between good and evil." The LORD was so very pleased that he declared he would give him also long life and riches. (1 Kings 3:5-15.)

The second story has to do with Solomon's astute understanding of human nature. Two women, living in the same house, had babies. One of the infants died. Its mother exchanged her dead baby for the living one. Solomon believed the story of the mother who claimed that this had been done, but he had to have proof. By his absolute authority, he called for a swordsman, and ordered that the living child be divided half and half. Instantly the real mother gave up. "No, let the other woman have the baby, do not kill the child," she cried. The other woman said to go ahead and divide it so. Thus Solomon gave to the true mother the baby that was hers. (1 Kings 3:16-28.)

Due to the fact that there was peace in his time, Solomon was able to enjoy a measure of prosperity that was completely unknown to the Jews. Through minor tariffs on various items of commerce, he was able to make himself a rich man. He lived lavishly according to the standards of his people and although his court was small beside that of Egypt or Babylon, it was glorious in the sight of his people, and that was what counted.

His technique in getting business and in keeping the peace was to marry the various princesses of the countries around and about. For each wife that he took unto himself, he sought to maintain family good will. This he accomplished by providing for them all lavishly, and by allowing them to do whatever they pleased. His greatest prize by these arrangements was Pharaoh's daughter. (1 Kings 7:8.)

For each of his wives he built a place for worship, according to her own particular religion. To keep his numerous wives happy was an effort on his part. What he did for others, however, he thought well to do for his own God, and thus it was that the famous temple of King Solomon was built. There had never been a building like it in all the history of the Jews, and it remains to this day the most cherished building of all religious history.

The story of the building of the temple and the fact that the stone that went into its construction came from quarrying right underneath it is fascinating within itself. But the fact that it was built of cedars that were portaged from Lebanon and were hauled by oxen to Jerusalem, and then were so hewn that they could be fitted into place, so that "neither hammer nor axe nor any tool of iron was heard in the temple, while it was being built" gives to the construction an air of mystery. (1 Kings 6:7.)

Although the temple was small according to our standards today (for it was only ninety feet long, thirty feet wide, and forty-five feet high), there was about it a magnificence that has received greater appreciation from the people than any other building that has ever been erected. Pure gold was used for the ceilings and walls, and even for the floor.

Symbolism became the key to the temple. Everything had some special meaning. Everything was so planned that the stairs stood for something; the length of this, and the height of that, the angle of this—all stood for something. And from that day to this, people have been seeking to decipher the various meanings because the very groundwork of Freemasonry had its inception in the building of that strange and wonderful house of worship.

The candlesticks, the snuffers, the table for the bread of the Presence, the basins, all magnificently done in gold, were the treasure of the people, and they marveled even as they saw.

Solomon dedicated the temple with a prayer that is preserved in 1 Kings 8:23-61. The LORD was graciously pleased with what Solomon said and did, and made covenant with him that if he walked in His statutes, and obeyed His judgments all would indeed be blessed for the coming generations. (1 Kings 9:2-9.)

Payment to Hiram, king of Tyre, for the materials that were used in the temple was in terms of the surrender of some twenty border towns in northern Galilee. (1 Kings 9:11.)

Twenty years were consumed in the completion of the structure (1 Kings 9:11) and it is reckoned that 10,000 men were occupied each month over this tremendously long period.

The queen of Sheba heard of Solomon's surprising reign and wanted to see with her own eyes if it was true. Thereupon she went to Jerusalem where she saw him. She marveled at his wisdom and was duly impressed with the grandeur of his court. (1 Kings 10.)

Solomon's end was timely. His subjects were spent with the heavy taxes which he laid upon them. His justice seems to have depended entirely upon his own cleverness and not upon any written law, and when he died, the means of justice perished with him.

His son, Rehoboam, was a weakling. Revolution met him and rent the kingdom in two so that it was never again united into a strong union.

Religiously Solomon leaves no monument save that of the temple. His ideas about God have not survived. He made no contributions as to the concepts about God or to the spiritual enrichment of the people.

Yet so long as men live upon the earth they shall speak of the wisdom of Solomon. So long as men dream dreams they shall recall the glory of the temple of Solomon. So long as clever men seek to pit their wits against the thinking of the multitudes there will be some soul who will raise his voice to say, "Solomon once said . . ." and there will follow a quotation from the lips of this sage of Israel.

Jeroboam

Father: *Nebat*

Mother: *Zeruah*

Place: *Palestine and Egypt*

Scripture: *1 Kings 11:20—15:34*

Solomon's reign was one of total autonomy. His was an iron hand. His policies were not too wise, inasmuch as he took from the people their economic independence by making them dependent upon public works projects in the form of the construction of magnificent palaces and temples. The records point to the distress of the people following the completion of these vast enterprises.

Unrest and unemployment offered the ripe opportunity for a political adventurer, Jeroboam, who should be remembered as Jeroboam I. This very talented military man saw the desire on the part of the people for new leadership, and he offered himself. Solomon had noticed his ability and had promoted him to be the ruler of the house of Joseph. (1 Kings 11:28.)

One day on his way to Jerusalem, he met Ahijah, the prophet, wearing a new robe. Ahijah took off his new robe and tore it into twelve pieces.

"Take ten," he said, "for you shall be the ruler of ten tribes of Israel."

Jeroboam was fascinated, and wondered when he would be able to come into such power, and he was told that it would

106

not occur in the time of Solomon but that it would follow upon the time of his death when his son would try to take over the rule.

Word came to Solomon of Jeroboam's ambitions for the throne, and Solomon sought to kill him, but Jeroboam fled to Egypt, where he made himself known to Shishak, the king of Egypt. Jeroboam waited for the death of Solomon before he tried to step into power, for the wise old king was far too astute to allow much thought for wresting the throne from him, or for dividing the kingdom so long as he lived.

When Solomon died, the time came to crown Rehoboam, Solomon's son, and the people made ready to gather at Shechem, which was a place of ready access. Some of the friends of Jeroboam sent him word to return to Palestine at once, and he came back to become the spokesman for the malcontents.

"Lower our taxes and we will serve you," Jeroboam said to Rehoboam.

"Give me three days to work out the details," he answered.

Actually what he did was to consult with his advisers. The old men said to ease up. The young men said to bear down.

Thus it was that at the end of the three-day period when Jeroboam came back to ask the answer from the king, he received the reply, "My father made your yoke heavy, but I will add to your yoke; my father chastised you with whips, but I will chastise you with scorpions." (1 Kings 12:14.)

Immediately Jeroboam took the message to the Northern tribes, and they went to their tents, which meant that they prepared for battle. Rehoboam sent his tax collector, Adoram, among the tents where he was stoned to death. As soon as the word of this disaster reached Rehoboam, he fled to Jerusalem where he arranged to muster troops to conquer the ten Northern tribes. But word came from Shemaiah, who was the man of God in Jerusalem, to say that this division of northern and southern Israel was the will of the Lord.

107

Rehoboam yielded to the word of Shemaiah, and decided not to attempt the fight to regain the seceding tribes. Thus, by careful timing and by doing the right thing at the right time, and by saying the wise and discreet thing, Jeroboam was able to effect a bloodless revolt and to make himself king of the ten Northern tribes. About 200 years later these became the ten wandering tribes, or the ten lost tribes of Israel.

Jeroboam established himself at Shechem which was the very place where he had delivered his ultimatum to Rehoboam in the name of the ten Northern tribes. He made a capital of sorts and ruled the people.

Very quickly, however, he saw that he would have to make some new arrangements about the religious loyalties of the people, for if they continued to make their pilgrimages to Jerusalem as the holy city, then their enthusiasm would change, and they would go back to their old ways. He had a metallurgist cast two calves of gold, strangely like the one that Aaron molded years before, and one he had set up at Bethel and the other at Dan as objects of religious worship for his people. Then he established a new priestly line, not from among the Levites, and this all became a sin and a reproach to the people.

All went well until there came a man of God out of Judah who disputed the authenticity of the worship before these idols. Jeroboam was at Bethel and saw and heard the whole thing, and he stretched forth his hand and commanded that the man should be held. A paralysis set into his hand, and the text says that his hand "dried up" so that he could not pull it in again. Immediately a tremendous fear came upon Jeroboam, and he begged the man of God to pray to God that his hand should be restored to him again as it was. The man of God prayed and the hand was restored.

One day Jeroboam's son lay sick, and the father decided to disguise his wife and send her to the prophet Ahijah who years before had torn his garments into the twelve pieces and had told him to choose ten. So the wife came to Ahijah; the old prophet was told by the LORD who she was, and he told her that the child should die because Jeroboam had failed to walk uprightly before the LORD. This was sad news. She returned to her husband, only to have the child die immediately upon her return.

For twenty-two years this strong man ruled in Northern Israel. His rule seems to have been wise for upon his death there was no revolution. The ten tribes kept their own identity through to the time when they fell at the hand of Sennacherib in 722 B.C.

Jonah

Father: *Amittai*

Mother: *Not known*

Place: *Mediterranean Sea, Palestine, Assyria*

Scripture: *2 Kings 14:25; Book of Jonah*

It was through Jonah, as a prophet in the Kingdom of Israel, that new concepts of God came to the Hebrew people. He declared that God would bless the Kingdom of Israel, and these things came to pass. (2 Kings 14.)

On the western strip of the Mediterranean Sea lay a little seaport town on the coast of Spain that bore the name of Tarshish, a place of no significance other than it represented, for Jonah, a flight to the uttermost part of the earth.

In 850 B.C. each village, town, and territory had its local god. The LORD was thought of as living in Palestine. Had not Solomon most graciously built a home for him? He was supposed to live in his house. Thus the idea was that to escape from Palestine would be to get away from God.

Jonah took passage for Tarshish, only to find that God was there—the same God who had called to him to go to Nineveh, which was far to the East, was now with him as he fled to the West. To be sure, God was in the storm, as Jonah interpreted it; God sent the storm to punish him. The seamen realized that something was amiss and cast lots to discover the offending member aboard ship. The lot fell to Jonah and at his suggestion they pitched him overboard.

110

"The LORD appointed a great fish to swallow up Jonah; and Jonah was in the belly of the fish three days and three nights."

Jonah became a changed man after he was released from the fish's stomach. He made plans for going to Nineveh, and there he preached so successfully that the whole city was converted. Men and women from every walk of life repented of their sins and responded heartily by outward demonstrations of their sincerity by fasting, and by appearing on the streets garbed in sackcloth. That any one man should be able to preach with such effectiveness is truly marvelous. But Jonah was not happy in the revival of religion that his preaching espoused. He had utter contempt for the repentance of the people of Nineveh.

He went over to a hillside opposite the city and prepared to watch the fireworks. You see, he had just said that God would destroy their city because of its wickedness and sin. Very well, then—let God pour on the liquid fire.

There he sat under a gourd vine, finding refreshment in the shade of it. The next day a worm came and ate at the roots of the vine, thereby destroying it. Then Jonah prayed for death because God had not done what he had said he would do. Jonah preferred death to life when God proved himself so soft-hearted as to forgive the heathen Ninevites. (The prayers of Chapter 2 and Chapter 4 are worth careful reading and analysis.)

God then made clear to Jonah that his love encompasses all peoples regardless of their entities or where they live.

Thus Jonah is able to give to the religious concepts of mankind the idea that God is not local but universal; that his interest in mankind knows no boundaries, but is *for all men everywhere.*

Amos

Father: *Not known*

Mother: *Not known*

Place: *Palestine*

Time: *Circa 787* B.C.

Scripture: *The Book of Amos*

The Northern Kingdom knew a period of prosperity. During the course of its history between the time of its founding under Jeroboam and its fall in 722 B.C., approximately two hundred years later, there were times when the land flourished, and when the people enjoyed many material benefits.

Judah to the South considered itself the true faith, and the true nation. The Northern Kingdom was forever the rebel band, and while this idea persisted all through the years, nevertheless the Scripture keeps rather accurate account of all that happened there. Each change of king is recorded carefully in terms of who was king in Judah at the time, and then when there is a new king in Judah, his reign is marked in terms of what year it may have been of the rule of the king upon the throne of Israel.

In just the same way the Scripture tells of the experiences with various men of God who sought to bring the people of the North back into their true relationships with God. Amos was such a man. He was really a herdsman who spent part of his time gathering sycamore fruit. There was no market for such fruit in Judah, and he traveled to the North where he vended his wares. That travel brought him into contact with these people, and caused him to see many of the differences between their ways, their conduct, and the teachings that he considered right.

In the little Book of Amos we see how he decried the situation that he found. In a veritable series of denunciations he voiced his dissatisfaction with the people.

Damascus, he said, would be punished
"because they have threshed Gilead
    with instruments of iron."
Gaza, he insisted, would be punished
"because they carried into exile a whole people,
    to deliver them up to Edom." This might indicate
that there had been a little traffic in human slavery.
Tyre, he declared, was to be cursed for having
". . . delivered up a whole people to Edom."
Edom was to be punished
"because he pursued his brother with the sword."
The Ammonites were particularly brutal in their dealings with prisoners of war, and they would be punished because they
". . . ripped up women with child." (Amos 1:13.)
Moab was to be punished because there the bones of the king of Edom were burned into lime. Even Judah shared in the wrath of the LORD
"because they have rejected the law of the LORD."
Israel was to be punished
"because they sell the righteous for silver,
    and the needy for a pair of shoes."

It was these points of injustice, these desecrations of humanity, that alarmed Amos and that caused him to raise his voice in denunciation. Amos has always been thought of as the prophet of justice. Just as Hosea emphasized the mercy of God, and as Jonah proclaimed the universality of God, and as Moses insisted upon the fact that God was a God of law and order, so this shepherd, who spent part of his time gathering sycamore fruit and vending it across the borders of his own land to the Kingdom of Israel, is to be remembered as a layman whose insistence was upon justice and moral right.

In five visions he pictured for the Kingdom of Israel the disfavor of God. The first vision was concerned with the harvest. The first mowing belonged to the government and the latter growth was the farmer's own. Amos saw God sending a plague of locusts to eat up the latter growth so that the people would have nothing. Amos persuaded the LORD to withhold this punishment as he did the fire that was promised in the second vision. In the next one God had a plumb line which indicated that Israel was being measured and found wanting and that God would pass by the people of Israel thereafter. Then Amos prophesied to the priest Amaziah that his family would be destroyed, his land parceled out, and Israel would go into exile. The last vision was of a basket of summer fruit which indicated that the time was ripe for Israel's end. Events proved that the end at that time was scarcely fifty years distant.

Through the whole book runs the compelling note of God's love for these people, and of his concern for their welfare. Although he punished them, he wanted them to return to him. While he saw their injustices and their falsifications, he loved them and wanted them to be an example of righteousness to all the world. It is this impact of God's love for the people that endears us to Amos, and to the message that he has sought to bring of God's concern for mankind.

Hosea

Father: *Beeri*

Mother: *Not known*

Time: *Circa 740* B.C.

Place: *Israel*

Scripture: *The Book of Hosea*

Out of the tribulation of real experience some of us learn that certain practices do not pay, learn that sin has its own curse, learn that righteousness and holiness have their own reward.

Hosea learned about God out of the experiences that he had with his faithless wife. Her name was Gomer, and seemingly she was an attractive woman. She bore Hosea three children, Jezreel (1:4), Loruhamah (1:6 KJV), and Loammi (1:9 KJV). Then Gomer became interested in certain lovers who began courting her, and very foolishly she ran away with them. They promised her all manner of happiness. When once she was away from home, her family, her husband, she learned that she was utterly at the mercy of the passion of these men, and they despised her.

"I will go and return to my first husband; for then it was better with me than now" (2:7b), she said. She was not a free agent, however. She was a woman in Israel, and in those days the wife was the property of the husband or of whatsoever man was able to hold her. Thus it was that she had to stay where she was, had to endure the situation, distasteful though it might be, and wait for the opportunity that would make possible her return to her home, and to her place as matron of her household.

Just what means she may have used for getting word to Hosea as to her whereabouts we do not know. This much the text does say, that Hosea rebought her for fifteen pieces of silver. (3:2.) He could have whipped her daily; he could have killed her; he could have put her into isolation. Any humiliation that he might have seen fit to employ would have been quite acceptable in the thinking of his time. She had run away from him, she had been false to him, and once he had her as his rightful possession again, any procedure would have been permissible.

What comes as the great surprise then is that he restored her to her place as his wife. He said to her kindly, "You must dwell as mine for many days; you shall not play the harlot, or belong to another man; so will I also be to you." (3:3.)

Thus it was that out of his personal experience Hosea was able to conceive of a parallel in the mercy and the graciousness of God. Hosea was able to say to the people of Israel that God was distressed that they had been sinful people, that they had departed from the simplicities of his ways, and that they had followed strange gods. Of Israel he cried,

". . . I will put an end to all her mirth,
        her feasts, her new moons, her sabbaths,
        and all her appointed feasts."

These were acts of idol worship. They were the feasts for the sensuous rites of Baal and Asheroth.

Hosea decried the deceitfulness of the people, the ignorance of the people, the shamelessness of the people. Each of these things weighed heavily on his heart. He wanted so much to see the people live uprightly.

In his own mind he knew that those who sowed the wind would reap the whirlwind. He knew that there was a balancing of justice in the heart and in the thought of God. What he knew more than this, however, was that God was a merciful God. Had not he himself shown mercy in the case of Gomer? Had he not been able to receive her back and to forgive her? Very well, if he had been able to do so generous a thing when he was a mere mortal, then God, who was so much greater, whose wisdom and whose character was so much greater than man's, would be able to forgive even more magnanimously.

Notice the way in which the idea repeats,

"For I desire steadfast love and not sacrifice;
     the knowledge of God, rather than burnt offerings."
(6:6.)

     "Take away all iniquity;
accept that which is good." (14:2b.)

". . . the ways of the LORD are right,
     and the upright walk in them." (14:9b.)

Elijah

Father: *Not known*

Mother: *Not known*

Time: *Circa Ninth Century* B.C.

Place: *Palestine, Israel*

Scripture: *1 Kings 17:1—2 Kings 2:11*

Elijah is called a Tishbite, which means that he was an inhabitant of Tishbe in Gilead. (17:1.)

Our first acquaintance with this fiery old man of the Scripture comes in his appearance before Ahab when he proclaimed "there shall be neither dew nor rain these years." He did not specify as to how many years it would involve, but he knew that a drought was a serious affair, and he knew that once he proclaimed that there would be such a curse upon the land he would have to hide, and he fled to the brook Cherith where he ate the scraps that ravens brought their young. (1 Kings 17:4.) This proved to be a sufficient haven for him until the brook dried up and he had to move.

His next adventure was with a widow in the little community of Zarephath. He had no money, he had no food; he found her gathering sticks, preparing her last meal, for she had exhausted her little supply, and she and her son were to eat their last bit of food, and then starve. Elijah persuaded the woman to feed him with this last morsel. This she did and by so doing she discovered that the supply was replenished, and she and her son and the prophet managed to live off the supply until the long drought ended. (17:8-16.)

Then the widow's son sickened and died, and in her distress she blamed Elijah. She thought that her son's death was a curse upon her. Elijah took the child and carried him to the little loft of the house where he himself lived. There he prayed and stretched himself three times upon the boy, and the LORD heard his plea, and the child was restored to life and health. When the prophet took him downstairs to his mother, she said, "Now I know that you are a man of God, and that the word of the LORD in your mouth is truth."

Meanwhile the years passed, the drought continued, and the distress of the people reached its greatest tension. Ahab, the king of Israel, divided the land and sent Obadiah to course through the land in one direction while he, himself, went another way to look for grass to keep the animals alive. Ahab believed that Elijah brought the drought upon Israel and only Elijah would be able to remove the curse.

Meanwhile the LORD directed Elijah to go to Ahab and on the way he met Obadiah. Obadiah fell on his face and told Elijah that he had been faithful to the LORD, that he had hidden a hundred prophets of the LORD, fifty in one place and fifty in another, and that he had taken care of them during the long course of the drought, and that he had done this unbeknownst to Ahab. Elijah assured Obadiah that he could return to Ahab and tell him that Elijah would be there shortly. Obadiah was none too pleased at the prospect of having to trust Elijah to come before the king, but he went back to Ahab and on hearing the news Ahab went to meet Elijah.

Ahab accused Elijah of causing the trouble in Israel.

"I have not troubled Israel; but you have," the old seer declared. He insisted that the trouble lay in the fact that Ahab had yielded to the worship of false gods. He asked that the people and prophets of Israel meet him at Mount Carmel and there he proposed a test.

119

" 'If the Lord is God, follow him; but if Baal, then follow him.' And the people did not answer him a word." He went on, "I, even I only, am left a prophet of the Lord; but Baal's prophets are four hundred and fifty men. Let two bulls be given to us; and let them choose one bull for themselves, and cut it in pieces and lay it on the wood, but put no fire to it; and I will prepare the other bull, and lay it on the wood, and put no fire to it. And you call on the name of your god and I will call on the name of the Lord; and the God who answers by fire, he is God." And to this the people gave consent.

Thus it was on Mount Carmel that Elijah had the two altars prepared, the one for the priests of Baal and the other for himself as the lone worshiper of the Lord. The priests of Baal did everything that they knew to do—they entreated Baal, and they cut themselves with swords—but no fire came.

At the hour of evening sacrifice he prepared the second altar, and actually had water poured over it, and when he prayed: "O Lord, God of Abraham, Isaac, and Israel, let it be known this day that thou art God in Israel, and that I am thy servant, and that I have done all these things at thy word. Answer me, O Lord, answer me, that this people may know that thou, O Lord, art God, and that thou hast turned their hearts back."

The fire came, the altar was consumed, and the people rose and slew the prophets of Baal. Then came the great rains.

When Jezebel, the queen, heard that her priests had been killed, she was furious, and declared that she would kill Elijah. He spared her that trouble by hurrying to Mount Horeb where he hid himself. There the Lord told him that he would show himself. Wind, earthquake, and fire were shown, but the Lord was not in these. Then came a voice. And the Scripture reads: "When Elijah heard it, he wrapped his face in his mantle and went out and stood at the entrance of the cave." It was in this "still small voice" that the Lord had seen fit to reveal himself. He told Elijah to select as his successor Elisha the son of Shaphat. Elijah cast his mantle on Elisha as a symbol of the passing of the prophetic blessing from the one man to the next. (19:19-21.)

Jezebel, meanwhile, ruled with abandon at the capitol. She knew that her husband desired a very favored vineyard that belonged to a man named Naboth and that Naboth would not sell the vineyard. She arranged to have Naboth killed, and then Ahab took the land he wanted.

Fearful as Elijah was that Jezebel would kill him, the old prophet came forth from Horeb, and denounced the murder of Naboth. "The dogs shall eat the flesh of Jezebel," he declared. This actually came to pass later (2 Kings 9:36) when Jehu overcame Israel and had Jezebel thrown from the window of the palace to the pavement of the street below.

Ahab's son, Ahaziah, became his successor. He was injured when he fell through a lattice in the palace in the upper chamber. Instead of sending for one of the prophets of the LORD, however, he sent for one of the priests of Baalzebub, the god of Ekron.

Elijah was sent to meet the messengers on their way to the priests with the word that Ahaziah would die. When Ahaziah heard this, he sent a captain and fifty men to get the old prophet but these men were destroyed by fire. He sent a second captain with a group of fifty. These, too, were burned alive. Still determined, he sent a third captain with a group of fifty. This time the captain entreated the prophet to spare his life and the lives of his men, and he assured Elijah that he would be safe. Elijah went before Ahaziah and told him that he would die because of his failure to honor the LORD. Ahaziah died, and Elijah was spared. (2 Kings 1:16-17.)

The end of the old man's life is as dramatic as any part of it. He was carried up into heaven in a whirlwind. (2 Kings 2:11.) He left his mantle to Elisha who very faithfully and nobly carried on the prophetic tradition.

Isaiah

Father:	*Amoz*
Mother:	*Not known*
Time:	*Circa 760* B.C. *to 690* B.C.
Place:	*Kingdom of Judah*
Scripture:	*Book of Isaiah; 2 Kings, chapter 18 and 2 Chronicles 26:22 ff.*

Several things are to be borne in mind in connection with the study of Isaiah. These were the sunset years of the Kingdom of Israel, that northern section which was by far the larger part of the Hebrew tribes which had broken away under the rule of Jeroboam and had maintained itself through the centuries since. Isaiah did not live in Israel. His home was in Jerusalem. He was under the rule of the kings of Judah, and there were four of them to be on the throne during his life.

Israel was weak. Its moral structure had been undermined by the idolatry and the unprincipled living and indulgence of the people. Judah, too, was weak. The very temple itself was neglected and Jerusalem had its share of idols. To the far east the Assyrian power was on the warpath in an expansion program. Tiglath-Pileser conquered Israel to the north, and arranged that Israel was to pay him tribute. Tiny Judah trembled knowing that it might be only a short while until Judah, too, would fall.

Unlike Elijah, Elisha, Amos, and the others of the prophets who were poor men, Isaiah was a man of wealth. He moved in court society, his influence was felt among the rich. He combined politics and religion. He felt that God was much concerned with the state of the nation, and his messages ring with that particular note.

Some scholars are of the opinion that there were more than one writer of the Book of Isaiah. The book divides itself into two separate parts, each of which has its own unique character and emphasis. The first part covers thirty-nine chapters and covers the history of the period, the circumstances of the nation that were disturbing the peace and the plenty of the nation. The second part, which covers twenty-seven chapters, is prophetic in the more majestic sense of the word. There is no portion of the Bible that is more beloved than this part is.

When Isaiah was a youth of some twenty years, he had the vision in the temple which stands as an unequaled experience to this day. "In the year that King Uzziah died I saw the Lord sitting upon a throne, high and lifted up," he said. There he saw the seraphim, there he heard the crying incantation,
"Holy, holy, holy is the LORD of hosts;
the whole earth is full of his glory." Out of this experience in the neglected temple, Isaiah found his prophetic voice. He might be a man of unclean lips, and he might dwell among a people of unclean lips, yet God would cleanse him and would use him as his mouthpiece to the people. He was to speak as never before man dared to speak that the word of the Lord might be known to the hearts of the people, that they might be redeemed.

Because he was himself so thoroughly persuaded that God is a moral being, he hated to denounce Judah for its sins. (1:5 ff.)
> Why will you still be smitten? . . .
> Your country lies desolate,
> > your cities are burned with fire. . . .

Hear the word of the LORD. . . .
"Bring no more vain offerings. . . .
       your hands are full of blood.
Wash yourselves; make yourselves clean;
    remove the evil of your doings
    from before my eyes;
cease to do evil,
    learn to do good. . . .
"Come now, let us reason together,
    says the LORD:
though your sins are like scarlet,
    they shall be as white as snow;
though they are red like crimson,
    they shall become like wool."

There is a note of universality in the words:

It shall come to pass in the latter days,
    that the mountain of the house of the LORD
shall be established as the highest of the mountains,
    and shall be raised above the hills;
and all the nations shall flow to it. . . .
. . . he may teach us his ways
    and we may walk in his paths. . . .
[He] shall decide for many peoples;
and they shall beat their swords into plowshares,
    and their spears into pruning hooks;
nation shall not lift up sword against nation,
    neither shall they learn war any more. (2:2-4.)

The impact of his words is as cogent today as when they were spoken,

Woe to those who call evil good
    and good evil,
who put darkness for light
    and light for darkness. . . .
woe to those who are wise in their own eyes,
    and shrewd in their own sight!

Woe to those who are heroes at drinking wine,
>and valiant men in mixing strong drink,
who acquit the guilty for a bribe,
>and deprive the innocent of his right! (5:20 ff.)

In an appeal to Ahaz, who was the son of Uzziah and the ruler to follow his father, Isaiah prophesied the coming of a new day, a new sort of ruler. He was very sure that Assyria would come and take Judah captive, that the country would be desolate, that "briers and thorns" (7:23) would be all that would grow upon the pleasant slopes of Judah. As to the coming of the new ruler he said, "Behold, a young woman shall conceive and bear a son, and shall call his name Immanuel." (7:14b.)

Notice these ringing words:
Woe to those who decree iniquitous decrees,
>and the writers who keep writing oppression,
to turn aside the needy from justice,
>and to rob the poor of my people. (10:1-2.)

Persistently the unfair practices of the people outraged the gracious prophet. Under the "new ruler," or the Messiah, he declared:
There shall come forth a shoot
>from the stump of Jesse,
>and a branch shall grow out of his roots. . . .
. . . with righteousness shall he judge the poor,
>and decide with equity for the meek of the earth; . . .
The wolf shall dwell with the lamb. . . .
The cow and the bear shall feed. . . .
>and the lion shall eat straw like the ox.

Isaiah was completely confident that they would be taken captive by the Assyrians but he promised,
. . . there will be a highway from Assyria
>for the remnant which is left of his people. (11:16.)

There is always the reassurance that God will save, will preserve this remnant.

Isaiah was persuaded that help would not come from Egypt. Egypt was too weak a nation to offer any protection to Judah or any other country or people. "The king of Assyria shall lead away the Egyptians captives and the Ethiopians exiles, both the young and the old, naked and barefoot." (20:4.)

Jerusalem itself was besieged during the life of Isaiah. The account is given in detail in Isaiah, chapter 37. This siege was broken, however, and the joy of Hezekiah was unbounded. Some time later, however, there came messengers from the king of Babylon, and very foolishly Hezekiah received the gift that they brought and showed them the wealth of the temple and the proud possessions of little Judah. (39:1-3) Isaiah declared that this represented a most unwise move, and that there would come a time when Babylon would seize Jerusalem. "All that is in your house, and that which your fathers have stored up till this day, shall be carried to Babylon; nothing shall be left, says the LORD."

The rest of the book was written after the fall of Jerusalem in 586 B.C. by a prophet called Second Isaiah who was possibly a captive. It offers words of comfort for people who are sure to suffer and is strongly Messianic in its purport. Some of its words are so ingrained in our thinking that we seldom stop to realize from just what source they have come.

Comfort, comfort my people. . . .
A voice cries;
"In the wilderness prepare the way of the LORD,
    make straight in the desert a highway for our God. . . .
Get you up to a high mountain,
    O Zion, herald of good tidings;
say to the cities of Judah,
    "Behold your God!"
Behold, the Lord GOD comes with might. . . .
He will feed his flock like a shepherd,
    he will gather the lambs in his arms,
he will carry them in his bosom,
    and gently lead those that are with young. (40:1-11.)

The promises rang with a note of hope that was a blessing to the hard-pressed, and gave assurance to those who were already captives from Israel:

"Fear not, for I have redeemed you;
> I have called you by name, you are mine. . . .
Fear not, for I am with you;
> I will bring your offspring from the east,
> and from the west I will gather you." (43:1b, 5.)
"I am the Lord, and there is no other,
> besides me there is no God;
> I gird you, though you do not know me, . . .
> I am the Lord, and there is no other.
I form light and create darkness.
> I make weal and create woe,
> I am the Lord, who do all these things. . . .
"Woe to him who strives with his Maker,
> an earthen vessel with the potter!
Does the clay say to him who fashions it, 'What are you making'?
> or 'Your work has no handles'?" (45:5 ff.)
In the Messianic passages we read,
Who has believed what we have heard?
> And to whom has the arm of the Lord been revealed?
. . .

He was despised and rejected by men;
> a man of sorrows, and acquainted with grief;
and as one from whom men hide their faces
> he was despised and we esteemed him not. . . .
All we like sheep have gone astray;
> we have turned every one to his own way;
and the Lord has laid on him the iniquity of us all. (53:1, 3, 6.)
"Ho, every one who thirsts,
> come to the waters;
and he who has no money,
> come, buy and eat!

Come, buy wine and milk
    without money and without price. . . .
"Seek the LORD while he may be found,
    call upon him while he is near;
let the wicked forsake his way,
    and the unrighteous man his thoughts;
let him return to the LORD, that he may have mercy on him,
    and to our God, for he will abundantly pardon. . . .
For as the heavens are higher than the earth,
    so are my ways higher than your ways
    and my thoughts than your thoughts. (55:1, 6-7, 9.)

"For behold, I create new heavens and a new earth;
and the former things shall not be remembered
    or come into mind. . . .
They shall build houses and inhabit them;
    they shall plant vineyards and eat their fruit.
They shall not build and another inhabit. . . .
They shall not labor in vain,
    or bear children for calamity;
for they shall be the offspring of the blessed of the LORD,
    and their children with them." (65:17, 21-22, 23.)

Jeremiah

Father: *Hilkiah, one of the priests who lived in Anathoth near Jerusalem*

Mother: *Not known*

Time: *Circa 640-587* B.C.

Place: *Judah, Egypt*

Scripture: *Book of Jeremiah; Lamentations of Jeremiah; 2 Kings 24:1 ff. and 1 Chronicles 24:3*

Since the days of Saul, Judah had been self-governing—it had blossomed under Solomon, split under Rehoboam, but it had maintained itself through the centuries. Now it was so far overshadowed by the might of Babylon that unless it played absolutely into the hands of the king of that great city, there could be no hope for peace or even semiself-government.

Called in a vision to be a prophet, Jeremiah felt keenly all the unpopularity of the message that he felt he had to deliver. He was a realist. He saw the hopelessness of the position of his nation, yet in the face of every displeasure and in the face of certain punishment from the people and from the king, Jeremiah hurled his God-given thunderbolts.

His life covers the span of the last five kings of Judah: Josiah, Jehoahaz, Jehoiakim, Jehoiachin, and Zedekiah.

The reign of Josiah seems to have been a period of relative quietude. Josiah followed a policy of friendliness to Assyria and of enmity toward Egypt. This was a clear-cut relationship, and seemingly a wise friendship. For twenty years Jeremiah shared in this period of peace. Then there arose in Egypt a new urge for expansion, with the result that an armed force was sent against Judah. King Josiah met the enemy in battle, where he himself was killed and where his army was defeated.

This rise of Egypt brought a new situation to Judah. Jeremiah felt that the power was much greater in Assyria. The unfortunate people were caught in the grip between the two contending nations. Josiah's son, Jehoahaz, ascended the throne, and for three months he ruled in Jerusalem, but Pharaoh Neco, the king of Egypt, would not allow him to reign. He sent an armed escort to Judah. They took the fledgling king to Egypt, and put him in prison. This was the last time that Jehoahaz ever knew liberty, or ever saw his country.

His brother, Jehoiakim, was set upon the throne, and ruled as a puppet power under Pharaoh Neco. It was during this time that Jeremiah began his more pugnacious preaching. He felt that the relationships with Egypt constituted an undesirable alliance for his people. Consequently he declared that God would send the Assyrians to take them and that they would be captives. His message was directed at the idol worship which Jehoiakim allowed and at the evils of current society. He did not hesitate to criticize the rule of the king. This met with immediate response. Jehoiakim sent to have him arrested, and the prophet would have been jailed immediately had it not been for some of his friends who tipped him off so that he was able to hide. From his retreat he proceeded to write out his denunciation of the moral and political policy. This he gave to Baruch who was one of his friends. Baruch took the message to the king, read it to him page by page, and handed each bit to the king who cut it with his penknife (36:23) and burned it in the fire by which he was warming himself.

What Jeremiah had the wit to foresee began speedily to come to pass. Out of the East came the armies of Nebuchadnezzar. Pharaoh Neco was of no help. Jehoiakim did the only thing that he knew to do. He agreed to a relationship of subservience to this faraway power, but as quickly as the armies withdrew he broke his agreement and sought to establish an independence that proved fatal to him. Just how he came to his death is not explained.

Jehoiakim's young son, Jehoiachin, was made ruler in his stead, but this rule lasted only three months, for Nebuchadnezzar came and took him captive to Babylon along with a veritable host of the citizenry of Jerusalem, among whom were Daniel, Ezekiel, and the well-remembered Shadrach, Meshach, and Abednego.

Zedekiah was established to rule in the little city of Jerusalem. This he did, but not too well. He tried to court the favor of the Egyptians; this was disastrous. The Babylonians came and besieged the city.

During the days of the siege Jeremiah tried to tell Zedekiah that his only hope for saving his life and the lives of his people lay in surrender to the Babylonians, but Zedekiah was furious and thrust Jeremiah into a cistern. "And there was no water in the cistern, but only mire, and Jeremiah sank in the mire." (38: 6.) Ebedmelech, the Ethiopian, appealed to the king to reconsider the case of Jeremiah. He then took old rags and a rope and threw them down to the prophet that he might pad under his arms, lest the ropes should tear his skin as he was drawn up.

The king called Jeremiah and asked him if he had any new word from the LORD, and he replied, "If you will surrender to the princes of the king of Babylon, then your life shall be spared, and this city shall not be burned with fire, and you and your house shall live. But if you do not surrender to the princes of the king of Babylon, then this city shall be given into the hand of the Chaldeans, and they shall burn it with fire, and you shall not escape from their hand." (38:17-18.)

Zedekiah knew that here was an unswerving sense of integrity, and while he hated the cruel truth that the aged seer prophesied, there was nothing to do but accept the sincerity of it. Thus it was that Zedekiah learned that he would be taken captive and the city would be burned with fire.

131

The story of the capture of the city of Jerusalem and of the slaying of the sons of Zedekiah and the putting out of the king's eyes is all told vividly in chapter 39.

With the conquest of Nebuchadnezzar the prophecies of Jeremiah were fulfilled,

> "This whole land shall become a ruin and a waste, and these nations shall serve the king of Babylon seventy years. Then after seventy years are completed, I will punish the king of Babylon, and that nation, the land of the Chaldeans, for their iniquity, says the Lord, making the land an everlasting waste." (25: 11, 12.)

Jeremiah opposed the plan for the remnant of the Judahites to go into Egypt. Speaking for the Lord, he said: "If you will remain in this land, then will I build you up and not pull you down, for I will plant you, and not pluck you up; . . . Do not fear the king of Babylon, of whom you are afraid . . . for I am with you, to save you and to deliver you from his hand. . . ." Then the prophecy adds: "If you set your faces to enter Egypt and go to live there, . . . the famine of which you are afraid shall follow hard after you to Egypt; and there you shall die." (42:10, 15, 16.) The people went to Egypt anyhow, and took Jeremiah with them. There they settled at Tahpanhes. (43: 7.) They did not obey the voice of the Lord. They offered incense to other gods, and particularly to the queen of heaven. (44:17.) Jeremiah denounced the people and insisted that God would send Nebuchadnezzar to overthrow Pharaoh Hophra, who was the king of Egypt. (44:30.) This was fulfilled even as he had declared.

It must be recalled that it was the distress of the people that prompted the writings by these men. They used the manuscripts to keep in touch with those who were in bondage in Babylon and with others who were practically in bondage in Egypt. Communication took the form of written documents. Thus necessity brought into being the written prophecies that we have in Ezekiel, Jeremiah, Ezra, and Nehemiah.

132

Daniel

Father: *Not known*

Mother: *Not known*

Place: *Jerusalem and Babylon*

Scripture: *Book of Daniel*

Daniel managed to leave behind him the memory of a life that was heroically lived under very trying conditions, for it was during his lifetime that the last of power that had been Israel's and which was then Judah's came to its end. What few citizens remained were taken as slaves into Babylon.

The rulers of Babylon used many methods through which they sought to "Babylonize" these strange people, yet Daniel and his companions remained true to the faith, and proved themselves loyal to God according to the light of their understanding of what was right.

After the manner of a Rhodes scholarship, fifty of the young princes of Judah were given educational opportunity, and were assured promotion under what we might call civil service. Everything looked bright for them. Daniel asked the chief eunuch if he might follow the diet of his forefathers, and upon the basis of a ten-day experiment ten Babylonian lads were fed the approved ration, while four Jews were fed pulse and water. Daniel and his three friends came through this period more ruddy of complexion, more sturdy of countenance than the Babylonians. So the chief eunuch then allowed them to continue on this strange vegetable diet.

Notice that the names of all four were changed to approved Babylonian from: Daniel to Belteshazzar, Hananiah to Shadrach, Michael to Meshach, and Azariah to Abednego. Rather interestingly, the new names stuck for the three companions, but we always think of Daniel as *Daniel,* never as Belteshazzar.

The first six chapters narrate the experiences of Daniel and his friends. They illustrate the superiority of the LORD over the Babylonian deities.

Chapter 1—The story of the diet of pulse and water.

Chapter 2—The story of Daniel's interpretation of Nebuchadnezzar's forgotten dream.

Chapter 3—The story of Shadrach, Meshach, and Abednego in the fiery furnace.

Chapter 4—The story of Nebuchadnezzar's dream of the great tree, and Daniel's interpretation of it.

Chapter 5—The story of Belshazzar's feast.

Chapter 6—The story of Daniel in the lions' den.

Each of these tales is one of heroic daring and of unequaled courage. In every one of them there is the realization that only by the very hand of God could these amazing deliverances occur. Each one is complete within itself and stands alone. They are all told in the third person because somebody other than Daniel wrote the life history of this strange and wonderful character. We see the young Daniel calling for the same foods upon which he had lived in the homeland as a boy. We see him as he interprets for the king the dreams which he does not understand and which he has forgotten. Then the scene shifts from Daniel to his three companions, as they withstand the public demand that they worship the image of the king. Even when they are thrown into the burning furnace, they remain true to the faith in which they have been reared. Daniel comes on the scene again. Few people would have had the courage to tell the king that he was losing his mind, yet Daniel dared to do that very thing, at the same time managing to hold his place through the period when the king was a raving maniac, eating grass like the beasts of the field, for seven years. Then we see Daniel in his old age. First we meet him at the feast of Belshazzar where the sacred vessels from the temple have been brought to use as ornaments upon the table of the king. We see he is called upon to interpret the mysterious handwriting which has appeared upon the wall. This Daniel does with the warning to the king that his health and power will be taken from him because he has proved himself to be a failure as the ruler of his people. Last, we see the new ruler who overthrows Belshazzar, but when he comes in Daniel is recognized for the sake of his splendid integrity, the nobility of his character and the utter dependability of his word. Then under Cyrus, those who are jealous of his power set a trap for him in this fashion:

Any man who worships any god other than Cyrus, or asks any petition of any other than Cyrus, will be cast into the den of lions, by order of the king. Daniel, however, dares to ignore this command completely. He continues to worship three times daily as has been his custom, with his face toward Jerusalem, and consequently he is cast into the den of lions. By the grace of God he escapes, and then the very men who plotted his end are thrust into the same den and are killed.

That is the portent of the first six chapters of the book. Here, however, the entire tenor of the message changes. Instead of being written in the third person, it suddenly becomes a first-person account. "I" did this; "I" saw that; "I" had the other happen to me.

Another characteristic of the remaining chapters is that everything is couched in highly figurative language. Daniel has visions of all manner of strange and amazing things. There are beasts like lions that have eagle's wings, and seem to emerge from the sea. Bears, leopards, and beasts appear like men. We are told that these strange beasts are in reality four kings. (7:17.) Then there emerge ten horns, and we are told that these are really the kings that shall arise. (7:24.)

The reader is aware that the author is trying desperately to say something that is not quite clear to us. We find ourselves wishing that we could understand. The little stories of the first six chapters were so simple. They could be read to a child, and, if once read, could never be forgotten.

Then we gradually become aware that there is a similarity to another book in the Bible where another writer speaks in a sort of double language, as if he is trying to say something and yet for reasons of his own is having to go at the truth of the business obliquely. Almost as an inspiration it dawns upon us that the similarity is to the Book of Revelation. Both books have the same general character, especially in the latter part.

We have been told that there was definite reason for John's hiding the burden of his message in the time of the persecution which the early Christians were facing when he wrote the Book of Revelation. What could have been the causes of trouble in the time of the writing of Daniel? Was it that Daniel was afraid? We read that he was absolutely fearless. Why then the hesitation about speaking forth whatever might be in his mind?

Our most painstaking and searching scholars assure us that Daniel did not write the book that bears his name. They say it was written approximately four and a half centuries after his death, by some unknown hero who generously concealed his own identity that he might bring hope and promise to his people. It was in that period of Hebrew history which followed the conquest of Alexander the Great when a concerted effort was made to make the whole world Grecian. This was an exceedingly effective movement for the very language of the world became Greek. Our New Testament comes down to us in Greek.

Every effort was made to mold the world's thinking after the pattern of that philosophy, that thought, and the customs of that people. None was more zealous than a certain tyrant whose name was Antiochus Epiphanes whose nickname became Antiochus Epimanes which meant "Antiochus, the madman." He used every device known to man to humiliate the Jews, and to obliterate the customs that Ezekiel, Isaiah, and Jeremiah had loved and fostered. Actually swine flesh was offered upon the altar, and we are told that offerings from the temple at Jerusalem were taken for the support of the worship of Zeus. Circumcision was forbidden, the feasts and ceremonials were denied, Grecian dances were done in the pavilion before the temple there in Jerusalem.

From the back country, however, a group of brothers, whose family name was Maccabees, desired a return to the simple customs of their forefathers, and the one way they knew to strike out against the Grecian culture was with the sword. Immediately the whole territory was afire with the main issue of the day which became the right of the Greek overlord, Antiochus, to force his will upon the people. This was accomplished by extreme measures. There were mothers who were crucified with their babies hanging from their necks, all because the mothers had allowed the circumcision of the infants.

Faithful Jews were driven from their homes, into hiding. People who had copies of the Scripture were subject to extreme punishment, often death. Thus those books that were "forbidden" came to be the canon of the Old Testament. In the midst of this terrific situation a book was "found" which bore the name of "Daniel."

Now read the book, and see for yourself the message that it brings. Six stories of heroism are presented, then the "revelation" which was perfectly clear to them that in "their time" there would be persecution, there would be hardship, but that through any and every circumstance, God would be with them and would deliver them out of the hand of their persecutor.

As a voice from the dead, this Book of Daniel came to assure the Hebrews that God would be with them, that he would save them even as he had saved Daniel and the three friends from dire and dreadful danger.

Few writers have more signally blessed their readers than the man who described the life of Daniel for his people in the hour of their most tragic need. The book reassured them, it helped to keep them true to the faith, it gave them hope and promise and helped to make it possible for them to survive.

Ezekiel

Father: *Buzi*

Mother: *Not known*

Time: *Circa sixth century* B.C.

Place: *Jerusalem and Babylon*

Scripture: *Book of Ezekiel*

In spite of the fact that a few thousand Hebrew captives were transported to Eastern Babylon and by all rules of history should have been absorbed into the larger population, the miracle is that they were not quickly drawn into the mass of the new peoples and forgotten. They were surrounded by hundreds of thousands of their conquerors who were eager to assimilate them into their own life and culture, yet they remained a peculiar people.

The difference that kept them a peculiar people during that particular period and that has marked them as distinctly a race from that day to this has been due largely to the work of one of the men who made the long trek from Palestine to Babylon. He was a priest (1:3) taken in with the captives and seems to have had no unusual training for his holy office. We know little about him other than as a dramatic teacher of his people.

For all of his realism and for all of the candor of his prophecies, Ezekiel was, at heart, as tender as could be. When he was told that he should decry the evils of the people, he went to the river of Chebar, where he sat down for a week and watched the people, listening to their accounts of why they did what they did. Then he understood. They were oppressed, they were captive, and it was a combination of economic necessity and political good sense that they should try to get along with their conquerors. Their lot was not easy. They were utterly at the mercy of the Babylonians. Ezekiel could see all of this.

Ezekiel was instructed in his prophecies through visions. The first three chapters picture his preparation for his work through the vision of the winged creatures and the wheels within wheels symbolical of the omnipresence of God and the vision of the eating of the scroll symbolical of his obligation to warn his people of their danger.

At the LORD's command, Ezekiel warned of the state of Jerusalem. He drew on a brick a picture of the city, hedged it round with implements of war, and attacked it. Then he lay upon one side for 390 days without turning to indicate the length of the punishment in years of the people of Israel. Then he turned to his other side and lay on it for 40 days to symbolize in years the period of time for which the people of Judah would yet be captive.

Then Ezekiel envisioned the destruction of the temple at Jerusalem. He described the desecrations practiced in the temple, the slaughter of the people, and the burning of the city. Then he told about the LORD's departure from the temple which signified that he was disappointed at its profanation but that it would still be a sanctuary for his people.

The LORD spoke to Ezekiel and told him that he was to remove his household goods as a symbol to the people that they were to be moved. Dire as these prophecies were, still through them rose the hope of restoration and freedom if they would leave off their idolatrous tendencies and their transgressions.

This promise culminated when the LORD told Ezekiel to get two sticks and to write on one "For Judah, and the children of

Israel associated with him"; and on the other "For Joseph and all the house of Israel associated with him." The two sticks were to be joined to indicate that the people of Israel would be brought back to their own land and united with the people of Judah into one kingdom.

Of all the visions, of all the dreams, of all the experiences that the strange seer had, there was none that brought more hope to his people than his vision of the restored temple. To the people it became the symbol of their restoration and the promise of their new land. The vision of the new temple (chapters 40 and following) was of greater proportion and of more splendid material than the temple which Nebuchadnezzar had destroyed.

"It will come, it will come," Ezekiel reassured the people. All would be well if they kept the commands of the LORD, and if they obeyed his precepts. They were to eat the LORD's food, they were to live according to the laws of the LORD, they were to keep themselves as a distinctive people. This they did, and all that Ezekiel prophesied came to pass.

With an emphasis upon the individual as God's unit in dealing with his people, we find a significant note in Hebrew prophecy. He wanted the people to know that each man was individually responsible before the throne of God. No man should bear the brunt of another's sin. No son should bear the curse of a wayward father, or father bow his back because of an unworthy son. All of God's dealing with mankind should be upon the basis of each man's responsibility.

This meant that Ezekiel was appealing for people, as individuals, to respond to the plea for them to become God's peculiar people. No one man's righteousness or unrighteousness was to be the guiding factor in another man's uprightness. Each was to answer singly before God.

140

Ezra

Father: *Seraiah*

Mother: *Not known*

Time: *Circa 400* B.C.

Place: *Babylon and Jerusalem*

Scripture: *Book of Ezra*

Ezra was a brilliant man, well established in favor with Artaxerxes whose place in history is known from secular writings as well as through the Book of Ezra. As a priest and as a scribe Ezra had gained for himself a place of recognition and of confidence. Generally we think of the Jews as having escaped from Egypt and having been led out from bondage under the leadership of Moses; but there was a second exodus, a second escape from bondage, and that was the one in which Ezra and Nehemiah figured in the period following the Babylonian captivity. The man who was the leader of the second escape was Sheshbazzar whom Cyrus, the governor of Babylon, commanded to rebuild the temple at Jerusalem. (5:13-16.)

The slow progress of this enterprise covers the major portion of the Book of Ezra. The various official documents were copied word for word in order that the causes of delay could be understood and both political and social difficulties could be thoroughly delineated.

Cyrus, in fulfillment of the prophecy of Jeremiah, decreed that the temple should be rebuilt at Jerusalem. (1:1.) A call was made for volunteers to return to do the work. (1:3.) A sizable group made the trek, and once they were there, they found themselves in the midst of those who had been left behind at the time Nebuchadnezzar had taken Daniel and the others captive some seventy years before. This group of "natives" came to offer to help rebuild the temple. (4:2b.) When their co-operation was scorned, they prepared letters to Artaxerxes who in the meanwhile succeeded Cyrus as the ruler of the land. They urged him to look up the past records of the Jews. They assured him that he would find that they had always been a cantankerous people, and that if they were allowed to go forward with the work they planned, it would be only a matter of time before they refused to pay taxes, and became a thorn in the flesh of the kingdom. (4:11-16.) Their letter received immediate attention at headquarters, and word came from Artaxerxes to halt the construction. (4:17-22.)

Things remained at a standstill for some while until Haggai and Zechariah, whose prophecies appear among the closing books of the Old Testament, aroused the people to action. As the work progressed, the governor wrote to Darius who was ruling by that time. He gave a full account of all that Cyrus had commanded should be done, and what had been done. He asked for Darius' word on how to proceed. Again the communication received prompt attention and authority was given to complete the temple project, and to supply necessary aid for the labor.

Although Ezra was not concerned with the construction of the rebuilding of the temple, he was sent with orders and credentials from Artaxerxes to be the ruling priest and the most learned guide for the people and to try to stabilize religious conditions in Jerusalem.

Ezra was by no means sent out empty-handed. He carried with him almost a blanket order on the treasury of the king. (7:11-28.) In addition, Ezra and all of his group of religious workers were tax exempt. (7:24.)

He brought with him all manner of parchments, rolls, and records, and it is believed that it was through Ezra that the compilation of this library we now know as the Old Testament took its form and early shapings. Ezra, the scribe, gathered every document that he could find, and gave them into the temple keeping. It was through this means that the education of the people advanced, and that the canonization of those books regarded as the sacred ones began. (Nehemiah 8:1 ff.)

The thing that upset Ezra most, however, upon his arrival in Jerusalem, was the fraternization that had taken place with the motley array of people who were there at the time of the return of the people under Sheshbazzar. Intermarriage had become common, and there were all manner of alliances and interchange of customs.

"This cannot be," Ezra said to himself. And he prayed about it, for he wanted the people to be one people, a peculiar people, a pure strain. He proclaimed before the people a mass divorce proceeding whereby all of the marriages with these "natives" were terminated. (10:10-11.)

There was weeping, there was heartbreak, there was profound sadness, but Ezra had determined that the severance should be effected, and what he had decided was done. Husbands and wives bade one another farewell, children wept upon their fathers' necks, and mothers and their babes were put away.

In the Book of Nehemiah we learn that Ezra taught the people.

For one thing they learned the meaning of the sabbath day (8:9-12); next they learned of the ancient custom of building little booths in which they were to live for a week. This they did, and found great joy in keeping the ancient tradition (8:13-18). They observed a fast together (Chapter 9). The thing, however, that revolutionized their lives and established them as a religious unit was the keeping of the tithe, the setting apart of the Levites for the holy office. (10:37.) There seems to have been some difficulty about keeping exact track of which

143

were of the Levitical descent, and for that reason the new priests were chosen by lot. (Chapter 11.)

Shortly after the dedication Nehemiah left Jerusalem for the court of Artaxerxes. Twelve years later he secured the king's permission to visit Jerusalem. He found things as bad as they were before the building of the wall. Tobiah was living in the temple, the Levites were not receiving their tithes, and people were intermarrying. These problems were by no means easy to solve. Nehemiah spent many a sleepless night. But he set about to put into effect the old laws and to establish the priests and Levites in their work.

Just such actions have been the reasons for the Jews being thought of as a race distinct and apart. Actually they are merely a religious group, but their insistence upon separateness has branded them as a distinct and a peculiar blood and kindred.

Nehemiah

Father: *Hacaliah*

Mother: *Not known*

Time: *Circa 400* B.C.

Place: *Babylon and Jerusalem*

Scripture: *Book of Nehemiah*

The temple had been restored at Jerusalem and in the far-away Babylonian palace Nehemiah, the cupbearer, felt within himself the urgings to be a part of the movement to bring Israel to its former greatness and to share in the strengthening of Jerusalem as the nucleus of all this.

When he heard of the frightful condition of the city, its broken-down and weakened condition, he wept. Artaxerxes commented on his depression.

Then in considerable detail Nehemiah described the condition of the city, and pleaded with the king to allow him to go back there to share in the rebuilding of it.

Possibly as much to the surprise of Nehemiah as anyone else, the king commissioned him to return to Jerusalem, to rebuild its walls, and to bring about as much of its restoration as possible. Artaxerxes gave him money and supplies for the work. (2:8.)

Nehemiah followed a very wise plan. He did not tell anybody what he was going to do until he himself had the opportunity to view the whole layout, and to make computations as

to the possibilities for rectifying the damage, and for completing
the entire project. It was by night that he went out under the
light of the moon to see what the status of the walls really was.
He looked at every detail, made his own estimates, and when
he had acquainted himself with the different sections of the
walls, when he knew who lived in each and every sector and
what approximate time it would require to complete the labor,
Nehemiah called the people together, and told them what he
intended to do.

The people responded to his plan immediately. They were
thrilled at the prospect of having a restored Jerusalem, a refuge from marauders who preyed upon them. They longed
for a sense of security. A great wall would give them this.

On the other hand when word reached Sanballat, a Samaritan, and Tobiah, a leader of the Ammonites, they laughed until
their sides ached at the very preposterousness of such an idea.
The walls of Jerusalem had been torn down for nearly seventy
years. They had "ruled the roost" in those parts for a good
while, and who was this Nehemiah that he should think he was
combination engineer, military strategist, and political organ-
izer? That he should accomplish so great a task was ridiculous.

Nehemiah proceeded immediately to the labor, apportioned
the responsibility by family, and arranged for the work in such
a way that the responsibility was allocated to "each one opposite his own house."

When Sanballat came with his troops to do battle with the
Jews, they (the Jews) were hard pressed. They were few in
number in the first place, they were short of supplies in the
second, and there was the immediate danger of these enemies.
Nehemiah realized that time had become a factor in his plans.
He arranged matters so that the work should go on from dawn
till dark. One shift stood guard while the others worked,
and sleeping was done by catnap. Nehemiah arranged for a
group of signals by which, at the sound of the trumpet, the people would know where an attack was being made and where
to rush for immediate action.

The men realized that there was danger. All they had to do was to look beyond the fragile walls, and see their enemies encamped round about. Merchants and moneylenders took advantage of them, for usury was common and when a man had no other security, he offered himself as such. Moneylenders were literally allowing the common men, the builders of the wall, the men who were fighting the fight that would give them new opportunity for commerce and financial standing, to enslave themselves. Nehemiah was horrified when he learned of it, and he called the noblemen and the moneylenders together, and berated them to their faces. He shamed them into canceling the obligations that the poor were under, and made them bear the brunt of the costs of the warfare and the construction that was being done.

Sanballat meanwhile attempted a new course of action. He sought to draw Nehemiah out of the city to meet him. Nehemiah was far too clever for any such trap and answered, "I am doing a great work and I cannot come down. Why should the work stop, while I leave it and come down to you?" (6:3.)

"So the wall was finished on the twenty-fifth day of the month of Elul, in fifty-two days." All the people realized that the "work had been accomplished with the help of our God." (6:15-16.)

A restudy of the ancient law of Moses was begun under the arrangement and the teaching of Ezra, the scribe. When the dedication of the walls was made, when the people realized that they were a peculiar people, that God had blessed them, and that he was blessing them specifically even in their own lifetime, they were awakened to a new spirit of joy and religious interest.

Esther

Father: *Abihail*

Mother: *Not known*

Time: *521* B.C.

Place: *Shushan and Babylon*

Scripture: *Book of Esther*

Esther was a waif, a displaced person as we would call her today. When her mother and father died, she was adopted by her cousin, Mordecai.

Esther grew to be a fantastically beautiful young maiden, and the time she came of age, a political situation arose in the kingdom that brought her into an entirely new orbit of life. Ahasuerus, perhaps better known as Xerxes, was the ruling power in Babylon. His was authority that was absolute, and after the manner of the Oriental potentates, his word was law. Word had gone out that Ahasuerus desired to entertain the rulers of the 127 provinces with a very special feast that should go down into history as one of the greatest feasts and festivals of all time. On the seventh day of the revelry Queen Vashti, whose beauty was far famed, was sent for at the king's order to present herself before these men. This would have been the sort of thing that only a prostitute would have done, and Vashti refused to obey the king's command. Xerxes was enraged and divorced her for daring to question a man's authority over his wife.

In those days, however, it was unthinkable that the king should be without a queen, so a beauty contest of national proportion was sponsored to find a girl who, for beauty of body and for personal charms, most delighted the king.

Mordecai saw in this situation the opportunity for which he had looked, and he entered his young charge, Esther. She seemed to delight all who saw her, and when her time came to go before the king, she proved to be more than satisfying. The king was delighted, and chose that she should be made queen instead of Vashti. (2:17.)

In the kingdom was a man of great power whose name was Haman. He was next in power to the king. Everywhere he went he was received with honor and people bowed before him with the exception of Mordecai, who refused to pay him such homage. This made him completely furious and he persuaded Ahasuerus to decree that all Jews be killed. The Jews, when they heard it, were grief stricken and Mordecai was distraught.

Something had to be done, and had to be done immediately. He sent word to Esther and asked her to plead for her race. She replied that she was not too strongly in the favor of the king at this time for he had not sent for her for a full month. (4:11.) Mordecai sent word to her that she must reconsider, for the situation was serious and that she must risk everything to gain favor with the king. Then very realistically he cautioned her that it would be of no avail for her to think she herself would escape. He reminded her that she, too, was a Jewess, and that she would perish along with the others. Esther answered Mordecai by asking that he and the Jews of Shushan declare a three-day fast praying for the success of her bold venture, for she feared to go before the king. "I and my maids will also fast as you do. Then I will go to the king, though it is against the law; and if I perish, I perish." (4:16.)

Esther presented herself before the king, and he extended his scepter toward her which meant that she might approach him.

Very graciously and with an appeal that must have delighted him, Esther invited the king and Haman to come to a dinner in her wing of the palace that very evening. The king accepted, and arranged for the invitation to reach Haman.

Both went and when the king asked her what she wanted, she invited them to a second dinner on the morrow, saying that at this later time she would reveal what she had in her heart. (5:8.)

Haman went home and bragged to his family about his wealth, his social favor, and expressed humiliation that this Mordecai still lived. His wife proposed that he build a gallows 75 feet high whereon this Mordecai should hang on the appointed day. This pleased Haman and he had the gallows built. (5:15.)

The king, however, could not sleep. He was restless and commanded that the official records should be read to him. There he heard of Mordecai having reported on some assassins who were planning to kill him.

"What was done in appreciation?" he asked.

"Nothing," was the answer.

Just then Haman appeared in the outer court.

"What shall I do for the man whom I delight to honor?" the king called to Haman.

Haman cleared his throat, and thinking that the king meant to honor him, he said, "Let royal robes be brought, which the king has worn, and the horse which the king has ridden, and on whose head a royal crown is set; and let the robes and the horse be handed over to one of the king's most noble princes; let him array the man whom the king delights to honor, and let him conduct the man on horseback through the open square of the city, proclaiming before him: 'Thus shall it be done to the man whom the king delights to honor.' "

"Very good," said the king, "go do all this to Mordecai."

Haman could scarcely believe his ears, but there was no chance for hesitation. He had to do what the king had said.

150

He had to lead the horse carrying Mordecai through the streets and his voice must have fairly choked as he had to say, "Thus shall it be done to the man whom the king delights to honor."

As soon as this was over it was time for Haman to go with the king to the dinner being given by Esther. When Ahasuerus asked what she wanted, she revealed to the king the fact that she and her people were being sold. She pleaded with him to spare her own life and that of her people.

The king demanded to know who had conceived such a dastardly crime against humanity.

Esther then exclaimed, "The enemy is this wicked Haman."

The king was shocked to realize that he himself was involved in the plot. He rose and went into the garden to think the business through, and while he was gone, Haman pleaded with the queen who had retired to her chamber. The king came in from the garden to discover Haman there and in fury gave command that Haman should be hanged upon the very gallows which he had designed for Mordecai.

Thus poetic justice was carried to its ultimate. Haman and all his sons were hanged. (9:13.) Mordecai was raised to the position which Haman had formerly held. Instead of being exterminated, the Jews were honored, and they thanked God for their deliverance in a feast that is still celebrated as the feast of Purim. (9:26.)

John the Baptist

Father: *Zechariah*

Mother: *Elizabeth*

Time: *Contemporary of Jesus*

Place: *Palestine and Arabian Desert*

Scripture: *Matthew 3; 4:12; 11:1; Mark 6:14; Luke 1:17; chapter 3; 7:18; John 1:6; 3:26*

The whole of our New Testament study is so thoroughly engrossed in the thought and the teaching of Jesus that it is well for us to stop occasionally to see that there are other men and women who were the people with whom he lived, and that it was they who figured very largely in his life. None has more definitely had a part than John the Baptist.

There was scarcely six months' difference in the ages of Jesus and John the Baptist. (Luke 1:26.) The preaching of John the Baptist immediately preceded the work and ministry of our Lord, and in the instance of Herod, we know that he thought that Jesus was actually John the Baptist come back to life. (Mark 6:14.)

The Gospel according to Luke opens with the account of the ministry of Zechariah's service in the temple, where he was serving as one of the priests. (Luke 1:8.) The marital disappointment of this man was made clear in the statement that his wife, Elizabeth, was barren. (Luke 1:7.) There in the very act of burning incense within the temple, Zechariah saw a vision, talked with the angel about the promise of a son, and asked for a sign of assurance that he should be given a child.

(Luke 1:18-20.) Zechariah was stricken dumb because of his lack of faith, and this dumbness remained with him until the child, John, was born. When the babe was circumcised (Luke 1:59), the question of his name was raised and Zechariah wrote "His name is John." Then his speech returned to him. (Luke 1:63-64.)

This child, born to a mother who was barren and aged, came to be the man apart. He lived in the wilderness. His diet was locusts and wild honey (Mark 1:6); his dress, animal skins and camel's hair. His manner of life seems to have been that of an ascetic for he was given neither to eating nor drinking (Matthew 11:18-19.)

John the Baptist was a man of unqualified character. His integrity was of sterling quality. When asked if he was the Christ, he replied: "No." He went on to say, "I baptize you with water; but he who is mightier than I is coming, the thong of whose sandals I am not worthy to untie; he will baptize you with the Holy Spirit and with fire." (Luke 3:16.) His ministry began as a washing ministry. He baptized his converts in the Jordan River.

This same idea is conveyed in the experience of those who asked John about the early ministry of Jesus which had begun to prove most successful. These people asked John which of the two men they should accept, himself or Jesus. "You yourselves bear me witness, that I said, I am not the Christ, but I have been sent before him. . . . He must increase, but I must decrease." (John 3:28, 30.) He conceived of himself as the "voice of one crying in the wilderness." (Compare Isaiah 40:3; Mark 1:3; Malachi 3:1.) John seems to have been willing to answer the questions of those who met with him and talked with him. He had a tremendous following. If we refer to Peter, Andrew, James and John, Philip and Nathanael as disciples of Christ, we may rightly refer to them as disciples of John the Baptist, because they were first his disciples and later disciples of the Lord. (John, chapter 1.) In fact, it was to hear John and to be baptized by him that Jesus went down to lower Jordan.

At the meeting of the two men, John showed himself to be a person of magnanimous spirit. He took the position of complete humility. "I need to be baptized by you, and do you come to me?" (Matthew 3:14) he says to Jesus. Again, in speaking of Jesus, he said, "After me comes a man who ranks before me, for he was before me." (John 1:30.)

Although he doubted the wisdom of his baptizing the Master, he proceeded to do it. And then he gave this testimony, "I saw the Spirit descend as a dove from heaven, and it remained on him. I myself did not know him; but he who sent me to baptize with water said to me, 'He on whom you see the Spirit descend and remain, this is he who baptizes with the Holy Spirit.' And I have seen and have borne witness that this is the Son of God." (John 1:32-34.) Each man seems to have seen in the other the qualities of greatness that were peculiarly his own.

John is a strange combination of gentleness and fire. The same man who conducted himself with uttermost self-efface-ment in the presence of Jesus, stood up before the people and screamed at them, "You brood of vipers! Who warned you to flee from the wrath to come? Bear fruits that befit repentance, and do not begin to say to yourselves, 'We have Abraham as our father'; for I tell you, God is able from these stones to raise up children to Abraham." (Luke 3:7-8.) And again at a moment in his preaching when his zeal carried him beyond the limits of discretion, he leveled his attack upon the throne, and denounced Herod for living with Herodias, who was rightly his brother's wife.

This same John was seeking with all the force of his preach-ing and of his persuasive power to make possible a new order of reformed life. When sinners came to him to ask him what they should rightly do, he answered them, "He who has two coats, let him share with him who has none; and he who has food, let him do likewise." (Luke 3:11.) When the tax col-lectors came to him, he told them to be honest in their levies. (Luke 3:13.) To the soldiers, John said, "Rob no one by violence or by false accusation, and be content with your wages." (Luke 3:14.) This was not just a matter of high-sounding preaching, it was an effort at immediate and practical application of the principles which he believed to be right and in accord with righteous morality.

According to Matthew the arrest and imprisonment of John became the deciding factor in the beginning of the ministry of Jesus, for Jesus started his preaching then. (Matthew 4:17.)

John heard about the work of Jesus. He must have wondered about it, for he sent his disciples to Jesus to ask him pointedly, "Are you he who is to come, or shall we look for another?" (Matthew 11:3.) Jesus then told them to reassure John that the blind receive their sight, the lame walk, the lepers are cleansed, the deaf hear, the dead are raised up and the poor have the gospel preached to them. This was like heavenly music to the ears of the imprisoned prophet. He awaited what justice or mercy was to come, and then by the irony of a fate entirely beyond his control he met his death.

It was Herod's birthday, and the fair daughter of Herodias danced for his guests. Excited to one of those extra generous offers that puppet rulers of the Orient have been wont to make throughout history, he said, "Whatever you ask me, I will give you, even half of my kingdom." (Mark 6:23.) She asked her mother what to request, and the mother said, "The head of John the baptizer." The deed was done, the head was brought on a platter, the voice of the wilderness preacher was silenced.

It was a cruel blow. Jesus heard of it through the disciples of John who first asked for his body to give it a decent burial. (Mark 6:29.) Then as sheep wanting a shepherd, they joined themselves to Jesus. (Mark 6:30.) The stage was set; Jesus' hour had come; history moved into a new dispensation.

Jesus said of him, "Truly I say to you, among those born of women there has risen no one greater than John the Baptist; yet he who is least in the kingdom of heaven is greater than he." (Matthew 11:11.)

Mary

Father: *Heli*

Mother: *Unknown*

Place: *Palestine and Egypt*

Scripture: *Luke 1:26, 38, 46; John 2:5; Matthew 1:18; Luke 2; John 2:1; Matthew 12:46; Mark 3:31; Luke 8:19; Matthew 27:56; John 19:25; Acts 1:14*

At the time of Elizabeth's sixth months of pregnancy when she was carrying John the Baptist, conception took place with Mary. (Luke 1:26.) Luke and Matthew both specifically mention the virginity of Mary (Luke 1:27 and Matthew 1:23 which is a quotation from Isaiah 7:14), both emphasize that it was while she was espoused to be married to Joseph that this conception occurred. Matthew makes it very clear that it was "before they came together she was found to be with child of the Holy Spirit." (Matthew 1:18.)

The story unfolds as follows:

Visit of the Angel: (Luke 1:28-38.) This was the pronouncement to the girl of what was to happen to her. "Hail, O favored one, the Lord is with you!" She would be the mother of a child whom she should name Jesus. She was told that her cousin, Elizabeth, "in her old age has also conceived a son; and this is the sixth month with her who was called barren."

Mary's Visit to Elizabeth: (Luke 1:39-56.) For three months Mary visited with her cousin, and when she was there Elizabeth bestowed a blessing upon her: "Blessed are you among

156

women and blessed is the fruit of your womb." This coupled with the angel's salutation is known in the Roman Catholic Church as the "Hail, Mary." The worship of Mary frequently overshadows the worship of Christ.

The Magnificat: (Luke 1:46-55.) The beauty of Mary's reply is unexcelled by any other words spoken by a woman in all the Scripture. She said to Elizabeth:

"My soul magnifies the Lord,
and my spirit rejoices in God my Savior,
for he has regarded the low estate of his handmaiden.
For behold, henceforth all generations will call me blessed. . . ."

Mary stayed until the time immediately preceding the birth of Elizabeth's child, and then she went back to her home.

Bethlehem: Each Christmas the story of the birth of the Christ child is read and retold all around the world. Matthew, chapter 2 and Luke, chapter 2 are the sources of the story. At the time of the taxing in the days of Caesar Augustus all the Jews had to go up to their own tribal cities to be taxed, so Joseph took Mary to Bethlehem. There she brought forth her first-born, wrapped him in swaddling clothes, and laid him in a manger.

Visit of the Shepherds: (Luke 2:8-20.) Joseph and Mary were hosts to the shepherds who came to tell them that they had seen a heavenly vision, that even as they watched their flocks upon the mountain sides, there appeared a chorus of angels praising God and saying:

"Glory to God in the highest,
and on earth, peace among men."

Presentation in the Temple: (Luke 2:21-39.) According to the custom of the Jews, both Joseph and Mary went up to the temple where they offered a pair of turtledoves or two young pigeons as a sacrifice of purification under the law. (Luke 2:

24.)   And while this was being done, Simeon the ancient prophet proclaimed in his prayer the unforgettable *Nunc Dimittis:*

"Lord, now lettest thou thy servant depart in peace,
according to thy word;
for mine eyes have seen thy salvation,
which thou hast prepared in the presence of all peoples,
a light for revelation to the Gentiles,
and for glory to thy people Israel." (29-32.)

Simeon told Mary that this child would be the most unusual in the history of all humanity:

"Behold, this child is set for the fall and rising of many in Israel,
and for a sign that is spoken against
(and a sword will pierce through your own soul also),
that thoughts out of many hearts may be revealed." (Luke 2:34-35.)

Visit of the Wise Men: (Matthew 2:1-13.) The wise men brought gifts of gold, frankincense, and myrrh. The time of this incident is not easy to compute. It seems that it was not concurrent with the birth night of the Christ although our Christmas teaching would tend to make it seem so.

Flight into Egypt: (Matthew 2:14.) This occurred as the result of a dream on the part of Joseph. Yet fortunately, the removal of the Holy Family meant their being saved, for Herod slaughtered all the male children "who were two years old or under, according to the time which he had ascertained from the wise men." (Matthew 2:16.)

To the Temple at Twelve: (Luke 2:42.) Mary and Joseph had taught the boy Jesus very carefully and thoroughly. He amazed the doctors of learning by his interpretations of Old Testament scripture. Rather interestingly, he rebuked his mother for not understanding, "Did you not know that I must be in my Father's house?" Mary kept all these sayings of her first-born in her heart. Mary had other children, specifically called by name in Matthew 13:55-58. Joseph died and Mary was widowed between the time that Jesus was twelve and the time that he began his preaching.

First Miracle: (John 2:1.) At a wedding in Cana in Galilee Mary came to the Master to tell him that the wine had given out at the wedding feast. She seemed to have been fully aware of his latent powers, and to have realized that he could do anything. Jesus scolded her for suggesting that he had anything to do with such mundane matters. Yet he proceeded to tell the servants to fill the pots with water which he then turned into wine.

Mary and her Children Follow Jesus: (Matthew 12:46-50.) Jesus seemed to feel that Mary and the family (apparently since the death of Joseph he had been the financial stay of the brood) should allow him to do his work without handicap. "Who is my mother and who are my brothers?" he exclaimed, and then answered his own question, "Whoever does the will of my Father in heaven." This was the third time that he rebuked Mary.

At the Cross: (Matthew 27:56 and John 19:26-27.) When Jesus was hanging from the cross, his mother was there. He looked down and saw her and said, "Woman, behold your son!" To John he said, "Behold your mother!" This was the unique way in which he asked the apostle to care for her who had brought him into the world, had nourished him, and had seen him through the course of his strange and wonderful life.

In the Early Church: Just how prominently she figured in the development of the early church is problematical. In Acts 1:14 we are told that she was with the company of those who had tarried at Jerusalem for prayer and to await the coming of power of the Holy Spirit. That she was interested and that she was a part of the movement is about all that can be said with assurance.

Joseph

Father: *Jacob*

Mother: *Not known*

Place: *Palestine and Egypt*

Scripture: *Matthew 1:19; 2:13, 19; Luke 1:27; 2:4*

Joseph was of royal descent from the issue of David, for at the time of tax gathering, Joseph was on his way to Bethlehem, the city of David. (Luke 2:4.) The angel who appeared to him in a dream to tell him that he should not hesitate to take Mary as his wife, who was already with child by the Holy Spirit, greeted him "Joseph, son of David." (Matthew 1:20.)

Joseph believed that God was leading and directing his life and his actions through his dreams. It was in his dreams that answers to his problems came, and whenever he was told what to do, he arose and followed the directions that had come to him in his sleep.

a. The decision that he should take Mary as his wife came as the result of a dream. Of course this was an important decision because otherwise Mary would have had no protection against the discriminations of society, and the Christ child would have lacked a home atmosphere with the balance of father and mother to guide him into normal growth and development. (Matthew 1:20-25.)

b. To act promptly upon the guidance of a dream as Joseph did when he was directed to flee to Egypt with his family was a brave thing to do. It meant pulling up stakes in

Nazareth without returning there to his carpenter bench. He simply fled with Mary and the babe to Egypt that he might insure the safety of the little one and the mother. (Matthew 2:13.)

c. At the end of approximately ten years of exile Joseph dreamed a new dream. This time he was told to return with the Holy Family to Palestine, and he did so in the face of fear and uncertainty. (Matthew 2:19.)

d. In another dream he was directed to turn aside from the environs near Jerusalem and to settle at the old homesite of Nazareth in Galilee. This came as welcome information, and it was there that he made his new home with a peace of mind he would not have felt anywhere else in Palestine.

That he should have believed that God was guiding and directing everything which came into his experience (whether it was through dreams that he had, or whether it was through the star which the wise men had followed, or whether it was through the vision of an angel chorus which the shepherds had upon the hillsides near Bethlehem) proves Joseph to be a man of faith. When he went into Egypt with the family, it was because he was led by the direction of God as he understood it. When he came back, it was the same.

We read of his observance of religious customs: "Now his parents went to Jerusalem every year at the feast of the passover." (Luke 2:41.) This was a long, arduous journey and expensive by their standards, yet it was part of Hebrew life and tradition, and Joseph kept these observances.

He figured only in the background of the incident at the time of the journey to the temple at Jerusalem when Jesus was twelve years old. He was concerned about the care of the boy, Jesus, and he heard all that was said, even as Mary did. The text specifically says, "And he [Jesus] went down with them and came to Nazareth, and was obedient unto them." (Luke 2:51.)

Jesus' impression of the ideal relationship between God and man was not as a mother and her son, but as a father and his son. This attitude is shown again and again in Jesus' remarks. Jesus loved Joseph and had unbounded respect for him or this concept would never have been crystallized as the ideal relationship. Consider the following quotations about God as the Father:

Matthew 5:16c	"give glory to your Father who is in heaven."
5:48b	"even as your heavenly Father is perfect."
6:1b	"then you have no reward of your Father which is in Heaven."
6:9b	"Our Father who art in heaven, Hallowed be thy name."
6:14b	"Your heavenly Father also will forgive you."
6:26c	"yet your heavenly Father feeds them."
7:11b	"how much more will your Father who is in heaven give good things to those who ask him?"
7:21c	"but he who does the will of my Father who is in heaven."
10:32-33	"So every one who acknowledges me before men, I also will acknowledge before my Father who is in heaven; but whoever denies me before men, I also will deny before my Father who is in heaven."

Jesus used this comparison from the first of his preaching to the last. He was always aware that this father-son, father-child relationship was wonderful in its capacity for mutual love and understanding.

Sometime between the visit to Jerusalem at the age of twelve, and the time of Jesus' going to lower Jordan to hear the preaching of John and to be baptized there by him, Joseph died.

162

Jesus

Father: *The Holy Spirit*

Mother: *Mary*

Place: *Palestine*

Scripture: *Matthew, Mark, Luke, and John*

In the Bible text there are four biographies—Matthew, Mark, Luke, and John. Each of these tells a slightly different story of this amazing person. Matthew and Luke record the incidents connected with his birth. The former tells of the visit of the wise men, and of their gifts of gold, frankincense, and myrrh. (Matthew 2:11.) The latter tells of the coming of the shepherds to the manger where the infant had been laid. (Luke 2:16.) All of it is woven into a pattern that is breathtaking in its beauty and that is eternally captivating in its wonderment.

As to the life of the infant Jesus, we know that he was born in Bethlehem (Luke 2:4), that the shepherds came and saw him there (Luke 28:18), that the Christ child was presented at the temple where he was circumcised as was the custom of the Jews (Luke 2:21 ff.), and that the wise men came (Matthew 2:1-12), that Joseph had a dream that he should take the babe and his mother and should flee to Egypt (Matthew 2:13 ff.), and that they escaped the slaughter of the children. (Matthew 2:16-18.)

Some ten years passed before the Holy Family returned to Palestine and when they did it was to make their home in Nazareth, a city regarded as of no significance in those days.

163

(Matthew 2:19-23.) This became the home residence of the family from that day. When the great holy days came, Jesus went with his parents to Jerusalem, and at the age of twelve he visited the great sacred city, there to confound the doctors, and to make his strange impression upon Mary and Joseph. (Luke 2:41-52.)

Marking the passage of time is not easy, but the key to it is found in such passages as Luke 2:1 where the statement appears "a decree went out from Caesar Augustus. . . . This was the first enrollment when Quirinius was governor of Syria" and Luke 3:1 where we read, "In the fifteenth year of the reign of Tiberius Caesar, Pontius Pilate being governor of Judea." There are records that make possible the chronology of these events, and through such sources it is determined that Jesus was approximately thirty years of age at the time that he went down to the river Jordan to be baptized by John. (Matthew 3:13-17.)

Ever so significant is the account that is given in the Synoptics—Matthew, Mark, and Luke—about the temptation of Jesus. Forty days he fasted and prayed and was tempted. When the period was ended, he was truly spent. These temptations come to all people in lesser degree, but it is accepted by even the bitterest foes of Jesus that his life was spotless and without sin. (Matthew 4:1-11.)

At the time of the imprisonment of John the Baptist, Jesus began his ministry in earnest. The import of his message bore an urgency for decision that men should become his disciples at all costs. His followers should forsake father and mother and should let the dead bury their dead. "Repent, for the kingdom of heaven is at hand." (Matthew 4:17.)

Almost immediately after his baptism, and before he was tempted, Jesus began to associate with godly men. He returned from his temptation to Capernaum which was near Nazareth, and there called Peter, Andrew, James, and John. These men became the nucleus of the group of apostles who followed him and who listened to his teachings, and who sought to apply

164

those teachings. There were twelve of them in all, "Simon, who is called Peter, and Andrew his brother; James, the son of Zebedee, and John his brother; Philip and Bartholomew; Thomas and Matthew the tax collector; James the son of Alphaeus, and Thaddaeus; Simon the Cananaean, and Judas Iscariot, who betrayed him." (Matthew 10:2b-4.) Each of these men made a name for himself, and each made a tremendous contribution to the meaning of Jesus' life, and to the understanding of all that he taught. Their questions to him become our questions, and the answers he gave to them become our answers. They were untutored men in the main. They were definitely not among the scribes who were the penmen of that day, nor were they trained in the schooling that characterized the priesthood, rabbinical and Levitical.

The first of all the miracles that Jesus performed was at the wedding at Cana in Galilee when the water became wine. The performing of this miracle represents Jesus' break with his mother's authority when he says, "O woman, what have you to do with me?" (John 2:1-11.)

After he was grown and had become a leader, Jesus made two trips to Jerusalem. The first of these is recorded in John 2 and 3. Here he cleanses the temple for the first time, and here he meets a member of the Sanhedrin whose name is Nicodemus. (John 2:3—3:21.) Some preaching and baptizing occurred on this first trip. (John 3:22 and 4:1.) It is interesting that Jesus himself did not baptize, but that his disciples did this, and that the baptizing took place at Aenon because "there was much water there." (John 3:23.)

When the Master went homeward to Galilee which was due north from Jerusalem and Judea, he passed through Samaria. This was a decidedly unorthodox move on his part. It was there that he met the woman at the well and there he converted her. (John 4:4-42.) That Jesus should dare to talk to a Samaritan was unthinkable in the strict code of those days.

At home in Nazareth he sought to establish himself as a preacher and a teacher, but when he stood up to read and dared

165

to associate himself with the Messiah, it was too much for the people and they cast him out of the city. (Luke 4:16-30.)

When the Master went to the house of Peter, he found that Peter's wife's mother lay sick of a fever, and Jesus healed her. Others who were sick pressed about him, and he healed them all. The Pharisees were furious with Jesus for performing an act of healing on the sabbath. (Matthew 8:14-15.)

As he went from synagogue to synagogue, Jesus found people all along the way who wanted help and succor. Jesus healed a leper (Matthew 8:2-3), he healed a paralytic (Matthew 9:2 ff.), he healed an infirm man at the pool of Bethzatha (John, chapter 5), he healed a man with a withered hand (Mark 3: 1-6), and demonstrated beyond the shadow of a doubt that he was blessed with power from on high to do such things. He spoke on the subject of fasting and its relationship to godliness (Matthew 9:14-17) and defended his disciples in the plucking of grain on the sabbath. (Mark 2:23-28.) These acts annoyed the Pharisees.

The Sermon on the Mount which embodied many subjects and so wide a range of spiritual content that it may well be thought of as a compilation of the emphases of Jesus' sayings, was delivered in Galilee, presumably at Mount Hebron. (Matthew, chapters 5, 6, and 7.) In these chapters are the Beatitudes, a reinterpretation of the commandments, the golden rule and the Lord's Prayer.

In little stories that can never be forgotten, Jesus illustrated his ideas. These were in the form of parables most of which have human characters as the basis of all the action and the plot of the narrative. One deals with a sower, another with a woman who was house cleaning, yet another with a man who had a vineyard. There are approximately forty of them which vary in length from fifty to 200 words. Actually they are a marvel of the storytelling art. Jesus knew that the people would remember the illustrations when they dealt with everyday situations, and for that reason he used them as he did.

At Nain when Jesus saw the dead son of the widow being carried to the burying ground, he stopped the procession and raised him from the dead. (Luke 7:11-17.) A second instance of resurrection is found in the story of Lazarus (John 11: 1-43) when Jesus raised him from the dead after four days in the tomb. This is symbolic of the resurrection of Jesus Christ.

Those people who were privileged to see Jesus walk on the water (Matthew 14:24-36) or who saw him still the tempest (Luke 8:22-25) or who were present when he brought sight to the blind and hearing to the deaf and caused the dumb to speak were amazed. They were right there, and they did not understand it. It is equally difficult for us to understand the miracles today.

It is distressing that any such people so fine in their observance of religion and so meticulous in their obedience to the code of ethics of their day as the scribes and Pharisees should have been so utterly lacking in the spirit of God's rule as Jesus conceived it. The scribes who read the law, and in the main interpreted it for the people, were given to very literal interpretations of it, but were in no wise concerned with the elements of mercy and justice, kindness and good will. Jesus berated them again and again, declaring that they were "like whitewashed tombs, which outwardly appear beautiful but within they are full of dead men's bones and all uncleanliness." (Matthew 23:27.) He said they were hypocrites (Matthew 23:29) and like snakes. (Matthew 23:33.) The scribes and Pharisees regarded him as blasphemous. They felt that he was utterly presumptuous in his claims. They regarded themselves as the champions of the law, and they felt that he desecrated the sacred commands with his unorthodox innovations.

The reasons for Jesus' crucifixion are many—his messianic claims, the diabolic element in human nature, his conflicts with the scribes and Pharisees over temple worship and the meaning of the law, and his seeming political aspirations as king of the Jews. All of these factors conspired to bring about the final stage of Jesus' life that we know as the Passion Week.

Sunday:	The triumphal entry into Jerusalem (Luke 19:29-44)
Monday:	The cursing of the fig tree (Mark 11:12-14)
	The cleansing of the temple (Mark 11:15-18)
Tuesday:	The fig tree withered away (Mark 11:20-25)
	Questions as to Christ's authority (Luke 20: 1-8)
	Teaching throughout the course of the day in the Temple area (Matthew 23)
	The widow's two mites (Mark 12:41-44)
	Gentiles seek Jesus (John 12:20-36)
	Conspiracy between the chief priests and Judas (Luke 22:1-6)
Wednesday:	No record
Thursday:	The Last Supper (Luke 22:7-30) (John, chapters 13, 14, 15, 16, and 17)
Friday:	The agony in Gethsemane (Matthew 26:36-46)
	Betrayal and arrest (Matthew 26:47-56)
	Trials (Matthew 26:57 through Matthew 27:31)
	Crucifixion (Luke 23:26-49)
Saturday:	The watch placed at the sepulchre (Matthew 27:62-66)
Easter Sunday:	The resurrection (Matthew 28:1-10)
	The report of the watch (Matthew 28:11-15)
	The disciples on way to Emmaus (Luke 24:13-35)

Final appearances and ascension (Luke 24:44-53)

Martha

Father: *Not known*

Mother: *Not known*

Time: *Contemporary of Jesus*

Place: *Bethany and Jerusalem*

Scripture: *Luke 10:38-42 and John 11:5-28*

Jesus' relationship with Lazarus, Mary, and Martha shows him working, talking, living with young people his own age. They ate together. They found fault with him, and did a bit of open and aboveboard friendly chiding that throws refreshing light upon the character of Jesus, himself, and immortalizes Martha, Mary, and Lazarus.

Mary, Martha, and Lazarus are mentioned in only two places in the scripture—Luke 10:38-42 and John 11:5-28. In the first of these Martha invited Jesus to supper. Martha prepared the meal while Mary entertained the guest. Finally when Mary continued to converse with Jesus, Martha's patience became exhausted and either half-chidingly or in earnest, she asked Jesus to bid Mary come and help her.

Jesus responded to Martha by saying she should not be anxious over household things. Mary was not shirking her responsibilities but choosing the good portion of life; that is, sitting at the feet of the Master Teacher to learn the meaning of existence.

169

In the second episode Lazarus was sick and Martha was probably doing the nursing. The sisters sent word to Jesus, saying, "Lord, he whom you love is ill."

Jesus did not go immediately to the aid of the sisters and the brother. He waited for two days and then told his disciples that he must go to Lazarus. Finally he made his way toward Bethany, and when he got near the place, Martha went out to meet him. Mary stayed behind in the house.

Martha chided Jesus for his delay. She knew where he had been and how long it should have taken him to get there. "Lord, if you had been here, my brother would not have died." There is something very direct about that. She was brokenhearted and evidently felt that Jesus might have exerted himself just a little more than he did. She went on, "I know that whatever you ask from God, God will give you."

Jesus' answer to this was more promising than even Martha dared to hope: "Your brother will rise again."

Martha answered, "I know that he will rise again in the resurrection at the last day." To this Jesus made the answer that rings in our ears with unforgettable significance: "I am the resurrection and the life; he who believes in me, though he die, yet shall he live, and whoever lives and believes in me shall never die." Then he asked Martha a question that might well serve as a poser for any of us and a test of our faith, "Do you believe this?"

Putting all her faith in one sentence, Martha answered, "Yes, Lord, I believe that you are the Christ, the Son of God, he who is coming into the world."

Then Martha went to Mary and said, "The Teacher is here and is calling for you." As soon as Mary learned that the Master had come, she arose and went outside the village to where he was. She fell at his feet and said, "Lord, if you had been here, my brother would not have died."

"When Jesus saw her weeping and the Jews who came with her, also weeping, he was deeply moved in spirit and troubled;

and he said, 'Where have you laid him?' They said to him, 'Lord, come and see.'"

Then "Jesus wept."

At the grave site Martha again became the central figure in the little drama. The Master proposed that the stone be removed from the mouth of the cave where the body of Lazarus had been laid. Martha cautioned Jesus: "Lord, by this time there will be an odor for he has been dead four days."

With her words of caution ringing in his ears Jesus said, "Did I not tell you that if you would believe you would see the glory of God?"

Then Jesus prayed and after the prayer called to Lazarus to come out of the tomb. Lazarus came out wrapped in the grave clothes.

A few days later shortly before the Passover Martha was again preparing supper for Jesus. While Martha prepared the food, Mary anointed the feet of Jesus with very costly ointment and wiped them with her hair. Judas Iscariot objected to this apparent waste of money and said the ointment should have been sold and the money given to the poor. Jesus tactfully saved the situation by saying, "Let her alone, let her keep it for the day of my burial. The poor you always have with you, but you do not always have me."

Mark, the Nephew of Barnabas

Father: *Not known*

Mother: *Mary (Acts 12:12)*

Time: *Time of Christ*

Place: *Jerusalem, Antioch, of Assyria, probably Rome and the site of ancient Babylon*

Scripture: *Acts 12:12, 25; 15:37; 2 Timothy 4:11*

It would seem almost preposterous that a reasonable picture of a man's life, his participation in events so long ago, could be built from such limited material as comes down to us from the verses mentioned above. This is true, yet we must recognize that Mark was caught in the midst of gigantic personalities, and in the stream of tremendous events. Thus while his life was significant in itself, it cannot be evaluated alone, but must be considered in connection with these other people.

Mark was the son of Mary, the sister of Barnabas, known as the "son of consolation" and one of the leaders of the early church. Mary generously made of her home a haven for the little Christian band. Tradition has it that the Last Supper was held at her house, when Mark was but a boy. It is possible that Mark listened and watched as the Lord served the emblems of the Last Supper. He may have seen the washing of the apostles' feet. Sometime in the night he went to look for

Jesus and discovered him being led away by the soldiers. Mark 14:51-52 reads, "And a young man followed him, with nothing but a linen cloth about his body; and they seized him, but he left the linen cloth and ran away naked."

The hatred between the Jews and the Christians became so bitter that Christians had difficulty in holding any form of employment. They managed only poorly in good times, and when famine came, as periodically it did, there was real suffering. Acts 11:27-30 tells of the distress within the city of Jerusalem, and to help in relieving that situation, Paul and Barnabas (who were working as co-pastors in the church of Antioch of Syria) raised funds to meet the need, and because there was no dispensing agent, they brought the relief monies to Jerusalem. Naturally Barnabas would go to the house of Mary, his sister. Mark was a student, a gentle soul, and he was thrilled at what he heard Paul say. Paul was a scholar, and it was as if they spoke a common language. "And Barnabas and Saul returned from Jerusalem when they had fulfilled their mission, bringing with them John whose other name was Mark." (Acts 12:25.)

When Paul and Barnabas planned their first missionary journey, Mark was included in the plan. Their route was across Cyprus where Barnabas' land holdings had been and where his family originated. For some unknown reason young Mark did not continue the missionary journey. "Now Paul and his company set sail from Paphos, and came to Perga in Pamphylia. And Mark left them and returned to Jerusalem." (Acts 13:13.) Now whatever it was that took Mark back to Jerusalem, must have been the deciding factor in the split between Paul and Mark, and between Paul and Barnabas, because Barnabas felt that the young man was justified; Paul did not.

A year later when the Jerusalem Council (Acts, chapter 15) had been held, and when Paul, Silas, Barnabas, and Mark had returned together to Antioch from that gathering, the question of a second missionary journey came up. Paul and Barnabas had shared in the first, why should they not go together on the second? This was not possible since Paul refused to let

173

Mark go because he had withdrawn from the first missionary journey. Thus Paul and Silas went together on the second missionary journey; and Barnabas and Mark went on a missionary journey of their own.

Just when the reconciliation between Paul and Mark took place is not known. Paul referred to him as a colaborer in Philemon 24, and he actually asked Timothy to send Mark to Rome to share with him in the work there. (2 Timothy 4:11.)

The other dynamic personality with whom Mark lived and worked was Simon Peter. We can reasonably assume that Mark saw Peter at the Last Supper, that he knew of Peter's denial of the Lord, that he was aware of Peter's marvelous ministry upon the day of Pentecost. Peter in his epistle referred to Mark as "my son." (1 Peter 5:13.)

There is strong belief among the scholars that Mark simply wrote down the events and the sayings as Peter gave them to him and as Peter preached them. What we have then is what Peter saw, and what Peter felt. Mark, who was the ready student, the scholar, found it easy to write it down, and did so, thus preserving for us the unforgettable record that is the basic gospel account.

Thus a man lived, a man worked, a man died. Because he worked with giant personalities, he was almost lost in the midst of them.

Judas

Father: *Simon*

Mother: *Not known*

Time: *Contemporary of Jesus*

Place: *Palestine*

Scripture: *Matthew 10:4, 26:14, 47, 27:5; Mark 3:19, 14:10, 43; Luke 6:16, 22:3, 47; John 6:70, 13:26, 18:2; Acts 1:18*

Judas Iscariot gets his name from the fact that he lived in the village of Kerioth. This indicates that he was actually the only one of all the twelve apostles who was not from the immediate province of Galilee.

What was this Judas like? What was his thinking, and what did he do? We have been so used to realizing that it was he who betrayed our Lord, we have been so trained into thinking of him as the man who was the basest of all men that we forget that the apostles themselves did not realize that he had any such weakness of character.

Judas was considered the very model of respectability and dependability. He was given the money box (John 12:6) which would mean that he handled all the money responsibilities of the disciples. It was he who dispensed what alms and benefactions they made, for you will remember that on the night of the Last Supper when Judas excused himself, the apostles thought that it was to go out onto the street to render some

175

mission of mercy. (John 13:29.) Judas ate with the others, walked with them, talked with them, slept with them. Matthew tells the story that when Jesus was bemoaning the fact one of them would betray him, they all asked, "Lord, is it I?" Judas asked this along with the others: "Lord, is it I?" (Matthew 26:25.) Jesus made no differentiation in his dealings with Judas and the others. He washed Judas' feet; he even gave Judas the communion.

Judas had been with Jesus day in and day out. He had seen the Master at work. He had shared in the hopes and dreams of the kingdom of God on earth. Surely he had sensed the Master's utter sincerity. Yet he betrayed Jesus for only thirty pieces of silver. If it was money that Judas wanted, he could have got it from the people whom Jesus healed.

It is probable that Judas was trying to force the Master to declare himself as the Lord of lords and King of kings. He may have been trying to put the Christ into such a position that there would be nothing else for him to do but to call upon his heavenly resources to get himself out of the predicament.

Judas must have loved Jesus. When he saw what the priests were doing to Jesus, he offered to return the money and begged them to release him. (Matthew 27:3-10.) He wanted to be done with the bargain. It was too late then, however, and the priests scorned him and snubbed him by every means within their power. Judas threw the coins on the temple floor and then went out and hanged himself.

The priests and elders looked upon the money that Judas brought back to the temple as tainted money. It is strange that they could have approved the policy of using temple money to buy a man's life, yet have reasoned that that same money, once it had bought a life, became untouchable coin because it was the price of blood.

Matthew

Father: *Alphaeus*

Mother: *Not known*

Time: *Contemporary of Jesus*

Place: *Palestine*

Scripture: *Matthew 9:9 and 10:3; Mark 2:14 and 3:18; Luke 5:27 and 6:15; Acts 1:13*

Matthew was a man of means, a collector of internal revenue for the Roman Empire, and there is every reason to believe that he was extremely prosperous. The tax gatherers were shrewd men, and they used every known device to squeeze the uttermost farthing out of the public. Matthew owned his own house; he was independent financially. Of all the men who subscribed to the responsibilities of discipleship, none sacrificed more in a monetary way than Levi who sat at the seat of custom.

Matthew had the ability to see in everything that Jesus said and did the fulfillment of the traditional promises of the prophets and seers of Israel. Through the course of their long and checkered history was the hovering hand of heaven; in all that they did and in all that their prophets and wise men did, there was the assurance that God was using them as in his supreme drama. Matthew was more keenly aware of this than any of the others. Somehow everything that he saw the Master do became a part of that larger pattern, a segment of the vast

177

mosaic of God's supreme handiwork. When it came to writing the Gospel, this man was able to take all of these incidents, to fit them into the traditions of their fathers so that they became a living link with the past—a long-awaited fulfillment of God's planning for the Jews.

Matthew seems to have been possessed of a photographic mind. Those things which he heard and which he saw were so vividly impressed upon his thinking that he was able to recall word for word and letter for letter the sayings of Jesus, the time and the place of those various happenings.

This unobtrusive gentleman, this man of talent and recognized ability in the financial world, has rendered a lasting service to us. He seems never to have crossed the Master in any word battles. He seems never to have risen as a gallant and valiant soul who offered his life for this cause or that, but he seems rather to have been one of the meek who do the business of the world and the business of the kingdom of God in a quiet and orderly manner, using his talents, such as they are, for the good of the kingdom, and for the perpetuation of the gospel.

Pontius Pilate

Father: *Not known*

Mother: *Not known*

Time: *Contemporary of Jesus*

Place: *Rome and Palestine*

Scripture: *Matthew, chapter 27; Mark, chapter 15; Luke, chapters 3 and 23; John 18:29 and 19:38; Acts 3:13; 4:27; 13:28; 1 Timothy 6:13*

Pilate, one of the least popular men of the scripture, was the Roman governor of Judea from A.D. 26 to 36. These were the years when Jesus' work was done. (Luke 3:1.)

It is undoubtedly because of the fact that all of our sympathies as believers are with Jesus, the Christ, that Pilate's very awkward political and judicial situation is condemned. "How could he have been so blind to the demands of justice and right?" we ask. Yet we know that the whole responsibility for the meting of justice rested upon the shoulders of the one man, and of him alone. We know that he represented Rome in matters executive, legislative, and judicial. He was the government.

Pilate was one of the lesser lights of Rome who was sent out to do a big job in the province of Judea. Tradition has it that it was only through the influence of his wife that he received the appointment at all.

His record shows a number of blunders in his dealings with the Jews. First, he marched his soldiers into the city of Jerusalem with little figures on the top of their standards. The soldiers regarded these as idols and worshiped them as such. To the Jews this was anathema, and they protested loud and long until the statues were removed. Then Pilate had tablets dedicated to the Emperor and set up in the castle across the street from the temple. This was violently opposed by the Jews who felt it was a desecration of the principles for which they stood. In the end Tiberius Caesar had to order Pilate to have these tablets removed from the castle.

The third thing that Pilate mismanaged was the erection of an aqueduct to bring needed water into the city of Jerusalem. On feast days the supply of water within the city was so low that the people found themselves in dire need. Pilate arranged for the building of this aqueduct, but instead of drawing upon Roman sources, or instead of persuading the priests to arrange for the payment of it, he arbitrarily demanded that the monies of the temple should be drawn upon to meet this needed city improvement. The people revolted, and the disturbance was quelled only after some bloodshed.

The incident of the trial of Jesus is the thing which all of us know most vividly, and yet that was not the thing which occasioned Pilate's recall to Rome. Some three years after the trial of the Master, there arose a disturbance about the supposed burial of various of the temple vessels on Mount Gerizim. When some zealous Jews went out to reclaim these vessels, Pilate slaughtered them. It was this unfortunate incident that brought about the recall of Pilate to Rome. When he arrived there, he learned that the Emperor was dead. Just what happened in the matter of the investigation of Pilate seems to be lost, but this much we know—Pilate was not returned to Palestine. Eusebius, one of the early Christian writers, says that Pilate committed suicide.

No account of these facts appears in the Bible text, so they must be gained from Bible encyclopedia and dictionaries.

Understanding between the Romans and the Jews was not easy. The very fact that Jerusalem was the religious center for a people who were scattered to the very limits of the empire seems to have escaped the comprehension of those in authority. One of the most astute of all the politicians of the time should have been stationed at Jerusalem, for it would have taken the wisdom of a Solomon to have managed the intricate political and social situation there. Palestine through all its long history has been a place of constant turmoil. It was then, it is now. It will be whenever this paper may be read years hence. Such is the nature of the struggle between the religious, political, and social forces that seek to express themselves there.

The accusers of Jesus did not enter the judgment hall because they did not wish to pollute themselves by being under the roof where there was leavened bread. It was the time of the Passover, and there would not be time for satisfactory ceremonial cleansing and they would miss participation in the sacred feast that was at hand. Thus it was that Jesus, the accused, was sent in before Pilate because he was under arrest, and as a prisoner was at the mercy of the soldiers who took him wherever he was ordered to go. On the other hand, the Jews who were not under arrest, but who were simply wanting to be done with Jesus, stayed outside the judgment hall. Thus Pilate shuttled back and forth through the doorway to talk first with Jesus and then with Jesus' accusers.

Pilate tried to release Jesus without offending the Jews. He used two ruses for this. First, he sent him to Herod Antipas. (Luke 23:6-12.) There is every reason to believe that Pilate wished to be done with what was to him a very definite annoyance. He was able to see through the unfairness of the accusations and he realized that here was purely religious bigotry, brought into conflict with a daring personality.

Second, Pilate tried to be done with the matter of Jesus by releasing one of the prisoners at the feast time. He thought surely that the triviality of the accusation against Jesus would be apparent to the people. When the people cried out to crucify Jesus, Pilate must have been among the most amazed of all. "I find no crime in him," he said. He was telling the whole truth then.

Pilate did not turn Jesus over to the Jews on the grounds that he was a malefactor. Pilate with his knowledge of Roman authority and the policies of the empire was too shrewd for that. He realized that when the Jews said Jesus had forbidden tribute, every man among his accusers was as much opposed as he to any small tax that Rome imposed; and for that reason, while it was not desirable from a Roman point of view that such grumbling at the paying of the Roman tax should be uttered, it was to be expected. Actually the suspicion of Pilate would naturally be toward the men who covered up their loathing of the tax, rather than against one who would speak out forthrightly against it. As to the accusation that Jesus was trying to make himself king, Pilate saw through that, too. He was philosopher enough to realize that Jesus' kingdom was, indeed, "not of this world."

What Pilate should have realized was that the only way he could defend Jesus would be to remove him to Galilee beyond the reach of the priests. What Pilate did do is history. He performed what seemed to him the symbolic act of freeing himself of all complicity in the death of one who he was certain was an innocent man. He washed his hands publicly before the people in order to disclaim any Roman responsibility for such utter disregard of justice.

Pilate failed to be strong at the very point where he could have won the lasting favor of all Christendom. On the other hand, if Jesus had been spared the cross, he would have been spared the resurrection, and to have been spared that experience would have impoverished our religious faith.

John

Father:	*Zebedee*
Mother:	*Mary*
Time:	*Contemporary of Jesus*
Place:	*Palestine and Asia Minor*
Scripture:	*Matthew 4:21; Luke 5:1-10; John 13:23, 19:26, 20:2, 21:7*

Two disciples of John the Baptist followed Jesus and were won by his simple and magnificent teaching. One of these was Andrew, Simon Peter's brother, and it is assumed that John was the other. John was a part of the gospel mission even from the first of Jesus' appearing in Palestine. This was at the time when Jesus was in lower Jordan where he had gone to hear John the Baptist and to be baptized by him.

John received a formal call to be a disciple of Jesus when the Master said to him and James, "Follow me, and I will make you fishers of men."

John was one of the three who were present at the raising of Jairus' daughter. (Mark 5:37.) He was one of the inner three at the transfiguration experience. (Matthew 17:1.) He was one of those privileged to be with Jesus in Gethsemane. (Matthew 26:37.) He was present at the healing of Peter's wife's mother. (Mark 1:31.) He was there at the time Jesus answered the questions concerning the prophecy regarding the overthrow of the temple. (Mark 13:3.) These were the things which Jesus wanted to keep pretty much as an inner-circle experience, and which he did not share with all of his followers. Yet John was there and John saw it all.

The general impression is that he was meek and mild, that he had little if anything to say. But he was a master fisherman in a trade that involved the handling of men far more than the handling of equipment. Jesus nicknamed him and his brother "Boanerges" which means "sons of thunder." (Mark 3:17.)

John was so incensed at the refusal of the Samaritan village to receive the Master that he proposed that the Lord call down fire and burn them up. (Luke 9:54.)

The other incident along this line that bestirred so much comment at the time it happened was the occasion when James and John came with their mother and requested that they should have the privilege of sitting to the right and to the left of the Lord when he should enter his heavenly kingdom. (Mark 10:35 and Matthew 20:20.) A study of these two passages will show that while it was the mother who made the request, actually it was the sons themselves who had got her to ask the favor which they themselves so very much wanted. The reaction of the apostles was one of rather strong rebuke.

At Jesus' request John went with Peter to make the arrangements for the Passover feast. (Luke 22:8.)

John came to Jesus to report that he had witnessed an unauthorized man "casting out demons" in Jesus' name. John forbade him to do this. Jesus said: "Do not forbid him; for no one who does a mighty work in my name will be able soon after to speak evil of me. For he who is not against us is for us. For truly, I say to you, whoever gives you a cup of water to drink because you bear the name of Christ, will by no means lose his reward." (Mark 9:38-41.)

On the night of the Last Supper when the apostles were together with Jesus, John was seated next to the Master, a place that was mutually acceptable to all concerned. The text reads, "One of his disciples, whom Jesus loved, was lying close to the breast of Jesus." (John 13:23.) Long years of tradition and

184

teaching have it that this was John. It was to John, then, that the question was directed as to who it was that should betray Jesus.

It was this disciple whom Jesus loved who was standing at the cross when the Master said to his mother, "Woman, behold your son!" and to the disciple, "Behold your mother!"

John was with Peter when Peter ran to the tomb on resurrection morning. (John 20:3-4.) John is mentioned again when he was fishing on the Sea of Tiberias with other disciples. (John, chapter 21.)

In 21:20-24 John described how the impression got abroad that he himself was not to die. He described himself as "the disciple whom Jesus loved," and as the one who "has written these things."

Three times John is mentioned in the Book of Acts:

1. When he was with Peter at the entrance to the Beautiful Gate of the Temple where the healing occurred for the man who had been lame from birth. (Acts 3:4.)

2. When he and Peter were hailed before the Sanhedrin and where they revealed very clearly that they were not highly tutored men according to the Hebrew tradition, but were devout, though unschooled, followers of Jesus. (Acts 4:5-22.)

3. As the companion of Peter on a preaching mission to the Samaritans where Peter and John were successful in causing those people to receive the gift of the Holy Spirit. (Acts 8:14-17.)

Peter

Father: *Jonah (Matthew 16:17)*

Mother: *Not known*

Time: *Contemporary of Jesus*

Place: *Palestine and Antioch of Syria and maybe Rome*

Scripture: *Matthew 4:18, 10:2, 14:29, 16:16, chapter 17, 26:69, 26:75; Mark 3:16, 8:29, chapter 9, 14:66, 14:72; Luke 5:1-11, 6:14, 9:20, 9:28, 22:54-62; John 1:35-42, 13:26, 18:17; Acts 1:15, 2:14, 3:12, 8:18, 9:32, 40, chapter 10, chapter 12, 15:7; Galatians 2:14; 1 Peter and 2 Peter*

"Peter" is a sturdy name. It stands as an affixed or Christ-given name, for the original was "Simon." (John 1:42.) Glimpses of Peter and Jesus very nearly constitute a complete life of Christ within themselves. Here are the major instances:

When Jesus went to hear John the Baptist preach and to be baptized by him, he met several of the men who were later to become his apostles. ~~Prime~~ among them were the brothers Andrew and Simon. Andrew was the first to meet Jesus and first to accept his Messiahship, but it was Peter whom we remember ~~most~~ clearly and who played the largest part in the scenes that ~~so speedily~~ followed. (John 1:40-42.)

Peter, Andrew, James, and John were all fishermen. It was near Capernaum ~~amid their own labors~~ on the Sea of Galilee that Jesus called them to apostleship. First he called Peter and Andrew, who left their nets to become "fishers of men." The same day, he called James and John, who just as promptly "left the boat and their father, and followed him." (Matthew 14: 18-22.)

Peter, his wife, and his mother-in-law lived together in their house near Capernaum by the Sea of Galilee. Jesus went into the house where Peter's mother-in-law lay sick with a fever. "He touched her hand, and the fever left her, and she rose and served him." (Matthew 8:14-15.)

Jesus was talking about the things he intended doing as the Messiah, that were definitely contrary to the things the Jews had always thought the Messiah would do. So very unexpected were the things Jesus said that "after this many of his disciples drew back, and no longer went about with him." It was a discouraging moment for Jesus, and he asked the apostles what they would do. Peter said, "Lord, to whom shall we go? You have the words of eternal life." (John 6:22-65.)

It was an expression of confidence when Jesus sent the brothers out and gave to them the responsibility of healing, preaching, and ministering to the people. These brothers knew each other and had perfect confidence one in the other. Jesus simply seized upon that natural understanding and made of the two a gospel team. (Matthew 10:1.)

When Peter saw Jesus walking upon the surface of the sea, Peter wanted to walk to Jesus, and to share in the divine manifestation. Jesus wanted him to share in it, and invited the apostle to come to him. When Peter began to sink into the waves, he called out, "Lord, save me." Jesus caught him and chided him about his lack of faith. (Matthew 14:28-31.)

It is easy to understand how Jesus would have wanted to know what the apostles themselves thought about him. His work had been so varied and the reactions of some had been so violent that Jesus simply had to know whether or not his teaching was taking hold, and whether he was being recognized as the Son of God. He therefore put the question indirectly at first, and discovered that some thought he was John the Baptist come to life, others that he was Elijah, or one of the prophets, returned. But this did not suffice. Jesus had to know what they themselves thought, so he asked, "But who do you say that I am?" Peter spoke up and answered, "You are the Christ, the Son of the living God." His statement rang with sincerity, and thrilled Jesus even as it thrills us. In great joy Jesus blessed

187

Peter and declared that this was a heavenly manifestation. (Matthew 16:13-17.)

It was with the inner circle of three, Peter, James, and John, that Jesus seems to have been most at home. Together they had gone to the top of Mount Hermon and there Jesus was transfigured before them. Moses and Elijah appeared and conversed with him. In a moment of unrestained exultation, Peter proposed that the Lord let him build three booths—one for him, one for Moses, and one for Elijah. Suddenly a cloud overshadowed them and a voice said, "This is my beloved Son, with whom I am well pleased; listen to him." When they looked again, Jesus was alone.

Jesus specifically charged them not to tell anyone of what they had seen and heard. (Matthew 17:1-9.)

At the Last Supper Jesus rose to prepare himself to wash their feet. Peter spoke up, "Lord, do you wash my feet?" Jesus answered that he intended to. Peter became firm, "You shall never wash my feet." But Jesus insisted, "If I do not wash you, you have no part in me." Then with love that made of the ceremony a glorious thing, Peter said, "Lord, not my feet only but also my hands and my head!" Peter took to heart the lesson that Jesus was trying to teach them, "For I have given you an example, that you also should do as I have done to you. Truly, truly, I say to you, a servant is not greater than his master." (John 13:1-20.)

From the Last Supper the Master took the apostles to the Mount of Olives where he selected Peter and James and John, and with these he went apart to pray. When he came back after a while he found the trio asleep. Jesus rebuked Peter, "So, could you not watch with me one hour? Watch and pray that you may not enter into temptation; the spirit indeed is willing, but the flesh is weak." Jesus left a second and a third time and returned to find them sleeping.

Then came the disturbance. Judas brought the soldiers, and Peter quickly did the one thing that bespoke a protest. With the best of intentions he made a gigantic arc with his sword, but being a fisherman and not a swordsman, he missed his opponent and slivered a piece of Malchus' ear. Another half inch and he would have missed the man altogether. Jesus told Peter to put up his sword, and healed the ear, as much as a protection to Peter as for the healing ministry that it represented. (Matthew 26:36-56; John 18:1-14.)

There is no doubt that Jesus knew better than Peter himself the nature of the man. When Jesus' trial and crucifixion were just ahead, Jesus said to Peter, "Simon, Simon, behold, Satan demanded to have you, that he might sift you like wheat, but I have prayed for you that your faith may not fail; and when you have turned again, strengthen your brethren." Peter answered: "Lord, I am ready to go with you to prison and to death." But Jesus said, "I tell you, Peter, the cock will not crow this day, until you three times deny that you know me." (Luke 22:31-34.)

The one blot upon the name of Peter came as the result of his being questioned when he was in the courtyard of the high priest's house. The Master had been arrested. Only within the last hour or so Peter had been humiliated when he tried desperately to lift the one hand that was raised in defense of the Master. Of all the apostles, only Peter and John ventured to follow into the very house of the high priest. There the servants began questioning him, and out of fear, Peter denied that he had any acquaintance whatsoever with Jesus.

The climax came when, at the moment of Peter's having three times denied that he knew Jesus, a rooster crowed. It reminded Peter that earlier this same night he had told Jesus that he would give his life for him, and that Jesus had replied that before the cock should crow, Peter would have denied him thrice. Peter looked toward Jesus, and at just that instant the eyes of Jesus looked straight into his own. It was too much for Peter. He went out and wept bitterly. (Luke 22:54-62.)

Very early on the morning of the resurrection day, it was Peter to whom the Lord appeared. Peter and the disciple whom Jesus loved ran with all haste to the tomb to verify the story

189

that the women had brought, telling of the Master's resurrection. There the Lord appeared to Simon.

During the forty days before the ascension, Peter and six others of the apostles were at the Sea of Tiberias when Peter announced that he was going fishing. At daybreak Jesus appeared and called from the shore, asking if they had any fish. They answered, "No." He told them to cast their net on the right side of the boat and then they were not able to haul it in for the catch. John said to Peter, "It is the Lord!" Instantly as if a spring had been set off within him, Peter grabbed his fisherman's coat and swam out, racing the boat to the shore that he might be the first to greet the Master.

They had a little meal of fish on the shore, and Jesus said to Peter, "Simon, son of John, do you love me more than these?" Many interpretations of this question have been given, but surely the comparison is with the fish as symbolical of material things rather than anything or anybody else. Then Peter received not once but three times the command to feed the sheep of Jesus. To all of us it stands as a thrice-repeated call to Peter to be a minister.

It is commonly taught that when Jesus said to Peter, "When you were young, you girded yourself and walked where you would; but when you are old, you will stretch out your hands, and another will gird you and carry you where you do not wish to go" (John 21:18), of course, he was prophesying that Peter would suffer martyrdom.

Peter's Ministry in the Early Church

Between the ascension and Pentecost was a ten-day waiting period in Jerusalem. During this time Peter suggested that a successor be selected for Judas to bring their number back to twelve. A man called Matthias was elected, but he seems to have been of little force, for that is the only mention that is made of him in all Holy Writ. (Acts 1:15-26.)

The experiences of the day of Pentecost were magnificent. When the baptism of the Holy Spirit came upon the apostles, Peter became the hero of the new Christian movement. This man who had been impulsive and almost ineffectual became, under the influence of the Holy Spirit, a giant of faith, a living voice of God, a man of irresistible power. When the visitation of the tongues came, and the apostles were invested with this new ability to speak in various languages, Peter, by an inspiration that far exceeded his own expectation, stood as the defender of the faith. This was prophecy fulfilled. This was the handiwork of God. The good, the bad, the cynical, the indifferent, all realized in amazement that this man meant what he said, and he was giving them the direction that God would have them to understand. Repentance, baptism, and the gift of the Holy Spirit became the postulates upon which he declared that they must become disciples of Christ. Three thousand came into the fellowship that day as a result. (Acts, chapter 2.)

Peter and John, seeing a beggar who had been lame from birth, ministered to him in the name of Jesus, and through their faith imparted to him the strength that healed the limb. This created a tremendous impression, and people came from every quarter to see the man and to hear Peter and John. Boldly they spoke of Jesus and the resurrection and of the power of the Holy Spirit. For this the rulers of the Sanhedrin arrested Peter and John and warned them specifically that they were not to preach or teach in the name of Jesus. Peter answered: "Whether it is right in the sight of God to listen to you rather than to God, you must judge." It was a bold statement, but they were delivering a bold message. (Acts, chapters 3 and 4.)

So impressive was the ministry of this man that people gathered by the thousands to hear him preach, to receive the healing ministry that he brought. Yet this very popularity worked against him, for the priests arrested him and John, and then debated as to how they would punish them. It was Gamaliel who persuaded them that the wiser policy would be to let time determine the rightness and the godliness of what Peter and John were preaching and teaching. It was Gamaliel's feeling that those things that are of God endure, that those things that are sham and pretense soon fade away. While

Gamaliel was able to keep the priests from killing the men, he was not able to keep the whips from off their backs, and both men were sorely scourged. (Acts, chapter 5.)

Simon, the sleight-of-hand artist, wanted to know how Peter healed the people. Peter declared that such techniques were not to be bought and sold, but that they were from God. (Acts 8:18-24.)

In Acts 9:32-40 Peter performed two additional miracles when he healed Aeneas who had been paralyzed for eight years and when he raised Tabitha after her death.

It is easy to lose exact chronology of the events, but somewhere during those busy years, Peter stepped aside as the head of the church, and James, the brother of our Lord, took his place.

Peter brought the gospel to the gentile household of Cornelius, thereupon breaking with the Judaizing element. (Acts, chapters 10 and 11.) In Acts, chapter 15, the story of the Jerusalem Council is given in detail. Were Gentiles to be included in the Christian fellowship without being required to comply fully with the Jewish law? Peter became the hero of the day. He remembered that the Lord had sent him to the household of Cornelius and that the baptism of the Holy Spirit had been given to that Gentile family, hence who was he to resist the Holy Spirit?

As to just what happened to Peter, there is no scriptural statement. He stands in his own right as one of the greatest of the early Christians. He speaks the thoughts of a common man, and seems to be subject to the frailties, the doubts, the misunderstandings of a thoroughly lovable and sincere person. That he was a writer is almost forgotten. First and 2 Peter are part of his writings; each is sound and of a noble spirit and concept. Then, too, the connection between Peter and Mark is lost sight of, yet it is commonly taught by the scholars that the Book of Mark may more rightly be termed the Gospel according to Peter because it so largely represents his reminiscences of the Lord and his preaching about him.

James, the Brother of Jesus

Father: *Joseph*

Mother: *Mary*

Time: *Contemporary with Jesus*

Place: *Palestine*

Scripture: *Galatians 1:19; Matthew 13:55; Mark 6:3; Acts 12:17; Book of James; Letter of Jude*

James, the brother of the Lord, was prominent in the work of the early church; he acted as the judge in the case where Peter and Paul were defending the reception of gentile believers into the fellowship of the church. (Acts 15:7-29.)

James is first mentioned with his brothers and sisters, the little family that Joseph and Mary had after Jesus was born. The passage reads: "And [Jesus] coming to his own country he taught them in their synagogue, so that they were astonished, and said, 'Where did this man get this wisdom and these mighty works? Is not this the carpenter's son? Is not his mother called Mary? Are not his brothers James and Joseph and Simon and Judas? And are not all his sisters with us? Where then did this man get all this?' And they took offense at him. But Jesus said to them, 'A prophet is not without honor except in his own country and in his own house.' " (Matthew 13:54-57.)

Jesus was probably only a year or two older than James. They grew up together, they played together, they shared in the same counsel of Joseph and Mary, and knew the same in-

193

fluences. It is also interesting to realize that many of the practical teachings of the little Epistle of James may have come from the lips of Jesus originally and that James may have written them down long afterward.

Just what part James may have played at the time of the work and ministry of the Master is lost in the telling of what Peter, the other James, and John did. They seem to dominate the scene. When Jesus was gone from them, when the early church was going through the long period of getting its feet on the ground, and when the details of administration pressed, James came into his own. Because of his very level-headed approach to the practical application of the principles of Jesus, the early church turned to him as the leader and the administrative head of the church itself.

When Peter returned from prison where he had been miraculously delivered, he went to the house of Mary, the mother of John Mark, where we believe that the Last Supper was solemnized. Peter was joyfully received. The text gives this description: "Motioning to them with his hand to be silent, he described to them how the Lord had brought him out of the prison. And he said, 'Tell this to James and to the brethren.' Then he departed and went to another place." Certainly James was figuring largely in the life of the Christians. Very probably they realized that he was in earnest about the things that Jesus had told him and possibly had not told the others, and thus the group turned to him repeatedly to get his opinions of what it was that Jesus meant.

A sentence or two from Paul's letter to the Galatians throws light upon the prominence of James at the time of Paul's own conversion. When he had retired to the wilderness of Arabia, and after things had cooled down about his own conversion, there came a time when he returned to Damascus, then Paul wrote (Galatians 1:18), "Then after three years I went up to Jerusalem to visit Cephas, and remained with him fifteen days. But I saw none of the other apostles except James the Lord's brother."

Whatever else may be said about this man lies in the field of conjecture. He must have lived through many an hour of hardship for his people. He must have stayed with them there in Jerusalem during the severe years of persecution and famine. It may, indeed, be true that through his influence and guidance the relief program of food and clothing was carried on. The records show that Paul promoted his cause in his preaching and that he carried much aid to Jerusalem whenever he went from Corinth with donations and personal representatives from the churches of Galatia, Asia, Macedonia, and Greece. (Acts 20: 4.)

Definitely this man James was one who believed that actions and words went hand in hand. It was right and good to make profession of faith, but there had to be a tie-up of real happiness and of some tangible work. Surely we will not be far afield if we assume that the interpretation James gave was his own sincere conviction of what every man who rightly called himself a follower of Jesus should think and do.

Paul

Father: *Not known*

Mother: *Not known*

Time: *Contemporary to Jesus*

Place: *Palestine, Asia Minor, Greece, Italy, and probably Spain*

Scripture: *Acts, Romans, 1 and 2 Corinthians, Galatians, Ephesians, Philippians, Colossians, 1 and 2 Thessalonians, 1 and 2 Timothy, Titus, Philemon, Hebrews*

Saul of Tarsus was educated in Jerusalem at the feet of Gamaliel (Acts 22:3) who is known to us as a liberal teacher in contrast with the conservative leader named Hillel. Taught by his father to be a tentmaker (Acts 18:3), Saul was ready to earn his living by his own hands if need be. He was, however, highly esteemed among the Jews because of his great zeal, his immense scholarship, and his unquestioned ability. Saul was a witness to the stoning of Stephen and consented to it. (Acts 7:58—8:1.)

Saul was a loyal Jew, and as such thought the claims of Christ were untrue. They were heresy of the most despicable order. Those who were in authority among the Jews sought to wipe out the teachings of this bold Galilean. They took what seemed to them the simplest and the most effective means, namely, to kill those who believed. It was in their work of completely wiping out these followers of Christ that Saul, desirous of proving himself a zealous and artful Jew, asked permission of the Jewish leaders to go to Damascus where some of the Christians were said to have found haven. He planned to go there to ferret them out, and "bring them bound to Jerusalem," which would mean, of course, sure punishment and death to them. (Acts 9:1-2.)

As Saul was nearing the outskirts of the city, at noonday, there appeared a light from heaven which utterly blinded him. He fell to the ground as one who has been stricken. Then a voice spoke and said, "Saul, Saul, why do you persecute me?" Saul answered, "Who are you, Lord?" Then came the reply, "I am Jesus, whom you are persecuting." (Acts 9:3-5.) This was the most significant moment in Saul's life. This was the voice of the Lord. To him it was his call to the service of his God and, without hesitation, Saul answered.

It meant the surrender of his place in Jewry. It meant that he renounced all his friendships and social claims, because the Jews have ever been a closely knit social group. It meant the acceptance of a new and untried faith in the ranks of which he would immediately expose himself to the very persecutions which he had been meting out with such vigor. Blinded, the man made his way to the house of Judas (Acts 9:11) where one Ananias came and blessed him and through God's grace brought back to him the sight which had left him. It must have been a trying moment for the Hebrew leaders in Damascus when they learned of Saul's about-face. Surely these Jews thought that if ever there was a traitor to the cause, Saul was that traitor. They sought him out as the most despicable of all their enemies.

After confessing Christ in Damascus Saul spent several years in Arabia. Later, when he reached Jerusalem, he spent a fortnight with Barnabas. There he saw Peter and James, the brother of our Lord. When they were completely talked out, they came to the conclusion among themselves that the thing for Saul to do would be to return to Tarsus, his father's city, there to wait until some opportunity for Christian service might afford itself. For the present certainly there was nothing that seemed to offer itself. For him to remain in Jerusalem would be to invite the wrath of the Sanhedrin and to bring some persecution upon the Christian community, with the possible chance for death to some of the brethren.

So Saul went to Tarsus. Exactly how many years it was that he stayed there awaiting the call to become the pastor of the church at Antioch is not determined, but it could have been in the neighborhood of nine years.

Antioch was the place to which Barnabas brought him, for it was Barnabas who remembered Saul and who seemed to believe that he would be of mighty service in drawing together the Gentile Christians and the Jewish Christians who were part and parcel of the Antioch congregation. (Acts 11:19-26.)

The distress, due to famine in Jerusalem and to the economic boycott of the Christians, reached such proportions that Saul and his congregation in Antioch raised some relief money for the alleviation of their troubles and, because they felt it the wisest policy, Saul and some of the brethren from the church came to Jerusalem together to oversee the distribution of the gifts that they had gathered for this purpose. (Acts 11:29-30; 25.)

First Missionary Journey

It was to Cyprus, the homeland of Barnabas, that Saul, Barnabas, and Mark came first on what is known as the First Missionary Journey. Barnabas had a nephew, John Mark, who accompanied the older men during their journey across the island. At Paphos, the capital at the eastern extremity, the conversion of the proconsul, Sergius Paulus, occurred. He became a convert due to the preaching of Saul. From this time on, Saul was known as Paul, the Roman form of the name. (Acts 13:1-12.)

At Perga, Mark returned to Jerusalem. This provoked Paul at the time, but there was nothing he could do about it. Later Paul refused to let Mark accompany him upon a Second Missionary Journey, and for that reason he and Barnabas severed company. (Acts 13:13.)

At Antioch of Pisidia, Paul and Barnabas founded a church. They were driven out by the conservative Jews. (Acts 13:14-50.)

At Iconium another church was founded. Paul and Barnabas were driven out by visiting Jews from Antioch of Pisidia. (Acts 13:51-14:4.)

When Paul and Barnabas arrived at Lystra, they found a lame man, and through God's grace they brought strength to his ankles and feet. The man leaped for joy, praising Paul and Barnabas. The villagers saw that a miracle had been worked in their midst, and they, supposing that the Greek gods had come down upon them, started to have a feast in their honor, actually calling Barnabas "Zeus," and Paul "Hermes." Paul dissuaded them from this intent, and managed to found a small congregation among them. What happened, however, when some of the trouble-raisers from Iconium came, is a sad critique upon human nature. These hard-hearted ones from Iconium insisted that Paul should be stoned, and those who had been ready a few days before to worship him, hurled stones at him with such force that they thought they had killed Paul, for they "left him for dead." (Acts 14:4-19.)

Paul rose up from the stoning and went with Barnabas to Derbe. Here they spent the winter of the First Missionary Journey. With the spring they retraced their steps through Lystra, Iconium, Antioch of Pisidia, then down the coast to Attalia where they took ship for Seleucia, and then to Antioch of Syria, thus completing the trip. (Acts 14:20-25.)

Antioch of Syria was the home base for the missionary journeys. Just who served as the pastor for the flock during the long periods of Paul's absence seems to have been lost. Peter and other leaders from Jerusalem as well as James, the brother of our Lord, had become exponents of the conservative party among the Christians. This group seemed to feel that the Gentiles were usurpers of the benefits of the blessings through Christ. Consequently trouble was in the offing among the Christians at Antioch. Paul sensed it, as quickly as he and Barnabas returned.

Peter and some of the brethren "withdrew and separated" themselves from eating with the Gentiles or having fellowship with them. (Galatians 2: 12.) Paul knew that this would not do, as he wrote, "I opposed him to his face." (Galatians 2:11.)

The conflict involving Peter and Paul became so heated that it was agreed the thing to do would be for them to go to Jerusalem, where the apostles and elders were gathered together. Before they left, however, Paul knew that something would have to be done about those newly professed Christians whom he had just established in the faith upon his recent trip. Therefore he wrote the Letter to the Galatians in the greatest possible haste. Here by every means that he knew to draw upon, he sought to persuade them to remain loyal to the faith to which he had called them. At Jerusalem, Peter recalled that he himself had been led by the Holy Spirit to go to the gentile household of Cornelius, that he had gone, and that he had witnessed there a visitation of the Holy Spirit upon those people who were not Jews at all but were Gentiles by every meaning of the term.

This Jerusalem Council, as it is called, decided that a policy should be followed among gentile Christians, and they should be asked to observe four restrictions only: that "they abstain from what has been sacrificed to idols and from blood, and from what is strangled and from unchastity." (Acts 15:29.) With this meeting and this decision behind them, Paul and the brethren returned to Antioch of Syria.

Second Missionary Journey

Rather quickly Paul felt the urge to revisit the brethren whom he had led into the faith there in Galatia. He talked the idea over with Barnabas who was willing and glad to go but who insisted that Mark be permitted to accompany them. Paul refused to be persuaded and Barnabas decided that he and Mark would go to Cyprus and revisit the tiny churches there.

Thus the severance of these two great Christians came about. Paul and Silas became new companions in mission work, while Barnabas saved his nephew to the Christian ministry by his own generous determination to befriend him.

Then Paul went to Derbe and to Lystra where he talked with Timothy, his mother Eunice, and his grandmother Lois. (2 Timothy 1:5.) Paul wanted the lad to accept the responsibility of Christian life service. Timothy responded immediately and became Paul's inseparable companion on the Second Journey. (Acts 16:1-3.)

At Beroea Paul formed the nucleus of a church, but he was driven out by the same element of conservative Jews who had caused the trouble in Thessalonica. (Acts 17:10.)

Undoubtedly Paul would have enjoyed being a part of that group of men of educational genius and power who resorted each day to the Acropolis at Athens, and he made one of the great addresses of all time before the Areopagus. While there were a few converts, the stumbling block for the Greeks was the resurrection, which they simply could not accept and without which Paul had nothing to preach. (Acts 17:15.)

Paul ministered at Corinth for a year and a half and it proved a very fruitful period. Here he made his home with those never-to-be-forgotten friends, Aquila and Priscilla, who were tentmakers and whom he took to Ephesus when he left Corinth. They later became the family around whom the Ephesian congregation was built. It was here in Corinth that Paul wrote the First and Second Letters to the Thessalonians. En route back to Antioch of Syria Paul visited Jerusalem. This ended the Second Journey. (Acts 18:1-22.)

Third Missionary Journey

Paul preached at Ephesus for two years. There he spent time each day in the hall of Tyrannus arguing, as the text puts it, although we today would likely call it teaching. It was during this period that Paul wrote the First and Second Letters to the Corinthians. Paul might have stayed indefinitely at Ephesus had it not been for the fact that one Alexander, a silversmith, raised a furor over the fact that the Christians were discrediting the benefits of the worship of Diana of the Ephesians which was the source of his own income and that of his fellow craftsmen. This grew into quite a disturbance. Paul felt that the part of greater wisdom would be to withdraw quietly from the city. He had been advising the churches all about that they should prepare for the accumulation of relief money for the Jerusalem brethren inasmuch as a new famine and period of hardship had come upon them. So Paul visited the churches in Europe, taking one representative from each congregation to carry the gift which that church had raised, and while his intention had been to sail to Caesarea from Cenchreae, he knew there would be danger involved, inasmuch as there were certain Jews who were lying in wait, and who would have seized some opportunity to throw him overboard. Thus it was that he and his party went by land to Philippi again, and then by boat to Caesarea and to Jerusalem.

While Paul was in Corinth this second time, he wrote the letter that we know as the Letter to the Romans.

It must be remembered, too, that en route to Jerusalem, at Miletus, Paul met with some of the brethren from Ephesus, among whom was one Eutychus, who went to sleep while Paul was preaching, and fell from the third floor to the ground. Everybody thought that he was dead, but Paul gathered him up, and said that he would be all right, and seemingly he was. (Acts 18:23—20:12.)

Paul's Arrest

The Greeks and gentile Christians that Paul had brought with him from those faraway places created quite a sensation in Jerusalem. All might have been well except for the fact that some of the brethren persuaded Paul that for strategy's sake he should share in the Hebrew ritual of the preparation for the feast. Paul agreed, and while he was in the temple, he was recognized and was accused of having brought some of these foreigners into the temple, thus defiling it. He was rushed outside the area, and would have been stoned had not some of the Roman guard observed the disturbance and come to his rescue.

What started out to be a rescue proved to be an arrest, for Paul was put in prison. There he defended himself by standing on his rights as a Roman citizen. His nephew, his sister's son

(Acts 23:16), brought him the news that some of the leaders among the Jews had determined to kill him. Paul appealed to the tribune for protection and arrangements were made for his safe conveyance to Caesarea. There, however, he was caught up in the entanglements between the Jewish courts and the Roman courts, and while he seems to have been perfectly safe, he was none the less a prisoner for two years.

No writing came out of this period so far as we know, but we have his famous defense before Agrippa which climaxed his stay in Caesarea, and which came at the end of his detention there.

Then came the long trip to Rome with its trials at sea, and when he finally arrived there, Paul was established in his own rented house under guard. There Paul wrote four letters—one to Philemon wherein Paul asked for the release of Onesimus the runaway slave; one to the Philippians in which he thanked them for the gift that they had sent for his care, and for the fact that they had sent Epaphroditus to help him; one to the Ephesians; and one to the Colossians.

It is to be noted that according to this outline of Paul's writing, 1 and 2 Timothy along with the letter to Titus are not included. Present-day scholarship points out that Paul would have had to write them during a period following his release from prison by Nero. It is supposed that Paul actually visited Spain, came back across the Mediterranean to Crete, visited Asia Minor, returned to Rome in disregard of Nero's insistence that Paul should never return to Rome. There he was put to death.

Luke

Father: *Not known*

Mother: *Not known*

Time: *Contemporary of Paul*

Place: *Palestine, Asia Minor, Greece, and Italy*

Scripture: *Colossians 4:14; 2 Timothy 4:11; Philemon 24*

It was while Paul was on his Second Missionary Journey and while he was being "forbidden by the Holy Spirit to speak the word in Asia" that he came to Troas, which was the point of embarkation in those days for all traffic that might be bound for Europe. There Paul met a physician whose name was Luke. A man of Macedonia appeared to Paul in a dream there in the city of Troas. This man said to him, "Come over to Macedonia and help us." (Acts 16:9.) Paul decided to go to the new continent with the message of the gospel, and Luke came to be drawn into the program of evangelism. It is here that the first of the "we" passages appears, and we may assume that Paul enlisted Luke's help in his missionary journeys.

Luke witnessed the healing of the demented slave girl, and he saw the cruelty dealt out to Paul for performing this very generous act. He not only witnessed the scourging of Paul and Silas, but he saw the spirit and the temper of these two men who, when they were beaten unjustly, held no malice; who, when they were thrown into prison, did not flee at the opportunity to escape in the night when the earthquake came, but stayed at their post and proceeded to convert the jailer who had treated them so unmercifully.

It was one thing to talk about a Savior of the world, but this was a demonstration such as Luke had never expected to see. Here were people who were acting with a generosity of spirit, and with a consecration of themselves such as he had never known existed. He could not help but realize that he was witnessing a new way of life, and he sensed a loyalty within himself to this new devotion and to this new movement which became for him a life dedication.

That things went tragically is all a part of the text. The magistrates of the city of Philippi asked Paul to leave. This was Luke's home, and it was with a feeling of tremendous embarrassment and heartbreak that Luke realized that such a man of God was out of place in the life of the community of which he was a part. He came to see that what happened in Philippi was but the pattern of what he might expect to happen anywhere that they went, for as quickly as they went to Thessalonica, they met with the same treatment. There the authorities asked Paul to move on. At Beroea the story was the same. While the message that Paul brought was one of faith and love, while the teaching that he gave was of a resurrected Savior and of a life of consecrated living, the reaction was never passive. There were those who accepted it gladly, there were others who just as violently opposed it.

We are led to believe that Luke was with Paul at the end of the Second Missionary Journey when Paul had the delegations from the various churches go with him to Jerusalem to distribute the largess which the churches had gathered for the relief of the hard-pressed Christians in Jerusalem. It is entirely possible that Luke stayed with Paul during the course of his imprisonment, waiting during the time that Felix refused to let Paul go and the time that Festus came and disposed of the matter by hearing Paul and then sending him on to Caesar for trial and final action.

Certainly the script indicates that Luke was with Paul when he was sent from Caesarea to Rome. This would mean that Luke was along during the days of the near-disastrous shipwreck. Then when Paul was in Rome itself, waiting another stretch of time before his appearance before Nero, Luke was there to serve him. (Colossians 4:14.)

Undoubtedly it was Luke's influence, quite as much as that of anybody else, that prompted the church at Philippi to aid Paul in the financing of his work, and in the sending of Epaphroditus to wait upon him. It may even be that the very fact of Luke's being there with Paul so constantly served as the reason for their great consciousness of the acute needs of the Apostle.

In the writing of the books we know as Luke and Acts, Luke intended not two companion books, but three.

The Gospel of Luke gives a wonderful picture of the life of Jesus. That he tells the story with a strong interest in the physical things that happened in the life of Jesus and in the lives of those who were closely associated with Jesus, is to be expected since Luke was a physician.

The value of what he accomplished in The Acts is beyond computation when it comes to telling us about the formation of the early church. There are those who promote the idea that Luke was very conscious of how many people were declaring that Peter was their great favorite, and that Peter was, because of that, the greatest of the apostles. What Luke seems to have done, according to these students, is to balance the work that Peter did with the work of Paul. Approximately half of the book is devoted to one, with the rest being given to the other, and with Paul getting the larger half, if such a thing is possible. Peter is shown healing a man who was lame from birth, Paul is shown doing the same; Peter gave his speech on Pentecost, Paul gave his in his defense before Agrippa. Peter is shown going to the household of Cornelius; Paul is shown converting Sergius Paulus.

Certainly The Acts constitutes the key by which the scholars weave together the pattern of the writing of the Epistles. Everything that happened had to take place against some chronological background, and it is The Acts that serves as the pattern for that study.

Thus as a man who was consecrated to the Christian movement, and as a writer who preserved for posterity the record of the times, Luke stands as a model for all Christians to see and to emulate.

Index